Crimes Against Nature

Jeff Sparrow is a writer, editor, broadcaster, and Walkley award–winning journalist. He is a columnist for *The Guardian* Australia, a former Breakfaster at Melbourne's 3RRR, and a past editor of *Overland* literary journal. His most recent books are *Fascists Among Us: online hate and the Christchurch massacre*; *Trigger Warnings: political correctness and the rise of the right*; and *No Way But This: in search of Paul Robeson*. He lectures at the Centre for Advancing Journalism at the University of Melbourne.

JEFF SPARROW

CRIMES AGAINST NATURE

CAPITALISM AND GLOBAL HEATING

SCRIBE

Melbourne · London

Scribe Publications
2 John St, Clerkenwell, London, WC1N 2ES, United Kingdom
18–20 Edward St, Brunswick, Victoria 3056, Australia
3754 Pleasant Ave, Suite 100, Minneapolis, Minnesota 55409, USA

Published by Scribe 2021

This project was assisted by the Cultural Fund of the Copyright Agency.

Typeset in Adobe Garamond Pro by the publishers

Printed and bound in the UK by CPI Group (UK) Ltd, Croydon CR0 4YY

Scribe Publications is committed to the sustainable use of natural resources and the use of paper products made responsibly from those resources.

978 1 914484 23 0 (UK edition)
978 1 950354 86 3 (US edition)
978 1 922310 70 5 (Australian edition)
978 1 922586 13 1 (ebook)

Catalogue records for this book are available from the National Library of Australia and the British Library.

scribepublications.co.uk
scribepublications.com
scribepublications.com.au

For Steph

Contents

The Guilty Party

In a famous passage, the labour organiser and folk singer Utah Phillips identified our whole planet as a crime scene.

'The earth is not dying,' he explained, 'it is being killed, and those who are killing it have names and addresses.'[1]

He's right. But it's not at all what we're usually told.

It's more common to hear that global heating stems from innate human greed, a vice for which we are all responsible.

We buy the wrong things, we eat the wrong food, and we don't separate our trash. Our collective rapacity drives the deforestation, the pollution, and, of course, the emissions of greenhouse gases, as industry groans and strains to keep us all satisfied.

That's the customary accusation, the 'common sense' narrative of climate change.

It's a frame-up, a calumny levelled to help the real culprits evade justice.

In reality, from the very first adoption of fossil fuels to the ineffectual negotiations on emission levels, climate change has been driven not by the many but by the few. A tiny coterie has used every weapon at its disposal to cajole, coerce, or persuade the rest of us to accept practices we never wanted and that we often resisted.

Whether we recycled or rode bicycles or turned off our lamps never made any difference to them.

According to the most recent Oxfam report, the twenty-six richest billionaires own as many assets as the 3.8 billion people comprising the poorest half of the planet's population.[2] Yet, despite the staggering inequalities of the current Gilded Age, we're still presented with narratives that flatten all responsibility for the crisis. In these stories, we're all guilty, with global heating and the environmental crisis more generally almost the inevitable consequence of human progress, as if homo sapiens were a kind of virulent disease.

To repeat, it's not true.

There's another history — a true history — that doesn't defame ordinary people, one in which the villain isn't humanity per se so much as a particular set of social and political structures that didn't exist in the past and needn't exist in the future.

This book presents a dozen interconnected essays offering a polemical indictment of capitalism's role in the climate emergency. It begins with a case study, showing how American car culture developed, not from a popular love for gas guzzlers, but as the result of a systematic corporate assault on sustainable alternatives. From there, it discusses the nature of nature, and shows how the destructive practices of our everyday life were forced upon us, often with tremendous violence. It tracks the campaigns deployed to normalise the war on nature, and explains how they will continue even as the planet's ecosystems decline and collapse. After a detour through a history of the Soviet Union and the environment movement itself, it argues that a better world remains possible, if we believe in our own ability to create it.

Climate researchers work in geological ages, studying vast periods over which they track changing conditions through sediments, dust, fossils, and other unimaginably ancient traces.

Yet they also tell us that time's running out — that, if we don't act at once, we risk broaching planetary limits and sending the world, via spiralling feedback loops, into a state from which it may never fully recover.

In other words, you're living through some of the most significant years in human history, with the decisions made in a desperately brief span weighing on the planet forever.

That awesome responsibility makes the attribution of liability for what's happened so far tremendously important.

At the very moment we need collective heroism and unparalleled determination, we're told that we're criminally worthless: mindless consumers obsessed only with material satisfaction, too lazy and stupid even to recycle, selfishly reproducing without thought to the ecological impact of our children, and almost genetically predisposed to selfishness and avarice.

Such accusations are paralysing.

The environmental crisis demands massive change. Part of that change pertains to how we think about guilt and responsibility.

You don't have to be the villain in this story. You could, in fact, be the hero — or, at least, one of them.

Let's see how.

CHAPTER ONE

The Hydrocarbon Explosion Engine

In 1995, the comedian Denis Leary recorded a track called 'Asshole', a song about an all-American guy who likes 'football and porno and books about war'. It concludes with a monologue:

I'm gonna get myself a 1967 Cadillac Eldorado convertible
Hot pink, with whale skin hubcaps
And all leather cow interior
And big brown baby seal eyes for head lights
And I'm gonna drive in that baby at 115 miles per hour
Getting' one mile per gallon
Sucking down Quarter Pounder cheeseburgers from
    McDonald's
In the old fashioned non-biodegradable Styrofoam containers
And when I'm done sucking down those greaseball burgers
I'm gonna wipe my mouth with the American flag
And then I'm gonna toss the Styrofoam containers right out
    the side
And there ain't a goddamn thing anybody can do about it …[1]

Today, Leary's rant takes on a special significance, since we all understand what Cadillac Eldorados do to the planet. A 2010 NASA study named motor vehicles as the US's greatest contributor to global warming. Cars consume great quantities of fossil fuels, and are notoriously energy-inefficient. They belch out greenhouse gases, and they do so without the counter-acting sulphates and other cooling aerosols produced by other industries.[2]

If you search for the phrase 'America's love affair with', Google autocompletes with 'cars' — with 'guns' a distant second. On best estimates, there are some 270 million cars currently in the US.[3] Ninety per cent of America households own at least one. Most own several. The low fuel prices produced by the fracking boom encouraged the use of SUVs and trucks, which now account for more than 60 per cent of vehicle sales.[4]

Obviously, Americans aren't the only people who drive. Throughout the developing world — especially South and East Asia — car ownership continues to grow. Chinese customers, for instance, bought some 28 million vehicles in 2019, a huge figure that actually represents a slight decline on recent trends.[5]

Nevertheless, the United States remains the spiritual home of car culture, the land in which a particular attitude to the automobile developed and was subsequently exported elsewhere. We're often told that car culture exemplifies the political dynamic of ecological destruction, a catastrophe resulting from the greed of the masses — in particular, the least educated of them. Many progressives say the planet is being wrecked by the public's insistence on driving, with those blue-collar assholes in their SUVs merely providing one gross example of broader human selfishness.

Interestingly, right-wing populists agree, although on the basis of a reversed set of priorities. They celebrate drivers as a core constituency, and laud car culture as a conservative philosophy, something to be upheld against liberal elitists. At a MAGA rally in early 2019, for instance, Donald Trump sneered at his opponents for their hostility to the vehicular choices of blue-blooded Americans. They wanted, he said, to get rid of aeroplanes and cows, and to mandate one car per family.

'And it's got to be of course an electric car, even if it only goes … 160 miles? What do you do with 160 miles …?' the president mocked. 'Darling, where do I get a charge?'[6]

Indeed, Trump's transportation secretary, Elaine L. Chao, had published, along with Andrew Wheeler (the acting administrator of the Environmental Protection Agency), a statement in *The Wall Street Journal* in which they pledged to roll back Obama-era vehicle-emission targets. They titled it, 'Make Cars Great Again'.[7]

Yet, before we accept Trump's presentation of car culture as evidence of innate working-class conservatism, we might note that Americans only recognised their supposedly longstanding 'love affair' with the automobile in 1961. In that year, Dupont (the owner of 23 per cent of General Motors) sponsored a TV documentary on the early history of American motoring called 'Merrily We Roll Along'. Narrating the program, Groucho Marx dubbed the public's relationship with cars a 'love affair' — the first time the comparison had been made.

After the screening, the phrase entered public consciousness, and never left it. (Nobody seemed to notice that it wasn't an affair any way you looked at it, as the cars couldn't love back.) The show introduced a term to millions of people, who subsequently forgot it was invented.[8] Dupont knew full well that ordinary Americans *hadn't* immediately fallen in love with cars. On the contrary, the car culture we take for granted, in the US and around the world, was formed only after a huge struggle by the auto industry, both against other less-destructive transport options and against the environmental consciousness of the public.

Precisely because the history of the car doesn't confirm the assholeishness of ordinary people, it makes a good introduction to some of the main themes in this book. Contrary to what many assume, the rise of car culture doesn't show how we're all guilty of environmental destruction. In fact, it shows quite the opposite.

As you would expect, the automobile's first enthusiasts in America were the wealthy — men able to afford an expensive and initially impractical machine. Part of the appeal of the private car was its exclusivity: for the first time, some people could travel much, much faster than others.[9] One motoring journal explained that its readers liked to speed so as 'to feel new sensations and juggle away the emptiness of a purposeless life'.[10]

The early vehicles were mechanically unreliable and limited as to where they could travel. The problem wasn't simply an absence of sealed surfaces. At the beginning of the twentieth century, the car could not dominate city streets in the way that it does now. Roads were public places. They belonged to everyone, and everyone used them, with busy streets treated like parks, open to all kinds of activities taking place simultaneously.[11] Elderly pedestrians walked where they chose, children used the street as their playground, and the onus was on the traveller not to hit others.

The first cars threatened this common understanding, and did so with great violence. In 1925 alone, cars killed 21,000 Americans, most of whom were on foot.[12] By our standards, that number might not seem huge, given that current highway fatalities outnumber the yearly toll in any war America ever fought.[13] But in the 1920s, when a child (and many of the casualties were children) died on the road, passers-by did not blame adults for lack of supervision, as they might today. They believed kids had a right to play. They denounced the drivers and their cars for selfishly monopolising a space that had previously belonged to everyone. The rich were widely seen as using the violence of their cars to terrorise working-class people off the roads. As early as 1906, Woodrow Wilson, the future president, warned, 'Nothing has spread Socialistic feeling in the country more than the use of automobiles. To the countryman, they are a picture of [the] arrogance of wealth with all its independence and carelessness.'[14]

Everywhere, people demanded action. In some places, they threw stones at passing cars — and, in one instance in Germany, piano wire deliberately strung across a busy street actually beheaded a motorist.[15] In America, boys threw rocks, bottles, and other missiles at cars with such regularity that one automobile magazine urged that stone throwing be made a felony offence.[16] Other protests were more sedate. In Cincinnati, in 1923, 42,000 people signed a petition demanding that cars be prevented from travelling more than 25 miles per hour.[17] Many experts and journalists agreed. In 1920, for instance, the newspaper *Illustrated World* argued for a device to physically limit cars to mandated speeds.[18]

Such proposals — and the early anti-car agitation as a whole — might sound foolish today. Certainly, the conventional narrative presents the modern automobile and its internal-combustion motor as inevitable, an invention embraced by the populace because of its innate usefulness.

But that's a retrospective projection.

During the last years of the nineteenth century, a variety of new machines had been invented, and many observers considered the 'hydrocarbon explosion engine' (as some writers styled it) less attractive than the alternatives. After all, of the 4,200 vehicles produced in the United States by 1900, fewer than 1,000 relied on internal combustion. The majority used either steam or electricity.[19]

Electric vehicles (EVs) seemed particularly promising. The first EVs could travel, on average, about 40 miles on a charge, a distance entirely adequate for early motorists constrained by crowded streets (and still greater than the daily commute of most Americans today). They were relatively slow, but they were also silent, accelerated quickly, and braked more effectively than gasoline vehicles. In a demonstration race in Philadelphia in 1908, a Studebaker electric vehicle showed it could outmatch a comparable internal-combustion vehicle in everyday conditions, partly because it didn't need to be cranked after each stop.[20]

Furthermore, as the inventor Pedro Salom explained in 1896, electric cars did not emit fumes, while their rivals 'belch[ed] forth from their exhaust pipe a continuous stream of partially unconsumed hydrocarbon in the form of a thin smoke with a highly noxious odor'.[21]

Alongside Henry Morris, Salom founded the Electric Vehicle Company in Philadelphia. The EVC produced a machine called the Electrobat, which featured a comfortable cabin modelled on a London Hansom cab and an electric engine with a range of twenty-five miles. While the EVC did sell its cars, it also offered an integrated transportation system, in which customers could hire an Electrobat by the day, the month, or the mile. The machines recharged at stations using an ingenious method in which batteries could be swapped within seventy-five seconds. In between trips, they were stored in a central location.

By January 1899, fifty-five cabs were in use. The company expanded to New York, a move seen as preparatory to a nationwide and even global operation, with, as one contemporary paper noted, 'a worldwide network of branch EVCs'. At its height, the EVC was the largest manufacturer of motor vehicles in the United States, and the largest owner and operator of them.[22]

But, like Uber and other ride-share services today, the EVC business model depended on rapid expansion, since the service could only become an option for everyday life if the company possessed a sufficient mass of vehicles. In the era of Teddy Roosevelt's 'trust-busting' rhetoric, the EVC's plans for a transport monopoly generated powerful opposition both from rivals and the public.

Then, in 1899, a newspaper showed that the company had underpinned its growth with a fraudulent loan. The revelation sent its stock plummeting, and the business collapsed.

Yet the disintegration of the EVC — a collapse so total as to wipe it and the Electrobat from historical memory — didn't reflect any technical inadequacy in electric vehicles. By all accounts, the Electrobat performed quite well. The business model might have failed, but the machine actually worked.[23]

Even by the 1920s, the individually owned internal-combustion engine was not the only game in town. To traffic-safety campaigners, the private car seemed contingent rather than inevitable. Why, they thought, should wealthy drivers be allowed to run down pedestrians at high speed when so many other options were available to them?

At that time, streetcars operated in most American cites, with the old horse-drawn trolleys increasingly powered by electric motors. By 1902, some five billion people trundled on streetcars in the US across about 35,000 kilometres of lines.[24] The system was safe, efficient, and much less polluting than the alternatives. Many people saw the expansion of streetcars as the logical way of moving the populace around a modern city, especially since, as one newspaper put it, 'the new problem created by the automobile' was 'will my child come home from school today alive and whole?'[25]

The campaign against the carnage wrought by cars coincided with a significant sales slump in 1923, despite the economy recovering from recession. Within the industry, manufacturers feared a saturation of demand. Those who wanted a car surely already possessed them — and many people, particularly those in cities, would neither need nor desire one.[26] Electrified public transport simply made more sense: why pay for your own dangerous and polluting vehicle when you could get everywhere you needed without the expense of ownership?

In the face of such dire prognostications, motoring interests rallied. Embracing the new field of public relations, they launched a prolonged crusade to reshape the population's views, in ways still being felt today. To overcome the outrage about pedestrian deaths, the industry created the figure of the 'jaywalker'.

In the mid-western slang of the time, a 'jay' meant a bumpkin or a hick, someone from a backwater unaccustomed to city etiquette. The word had previously been applied to 'jay drivers', hayseeds who didn't understand that, in the bustling metropolis, they couldn't use their carriages as they did in the boondocks.[27]

In the 1920s, dealers and auto clubs began applying 'jaywalker' to those pedestrians who still upheld the customary right to share the road. Local car firms paid boy scouts to distribute cards explaining the concept of jaywalking to passers-by, while the American Automobile Association promoted 'safety patrols' to warn children off the street. In many places, the industry staged elaborate pageants to ridicule jaywalkers. In a demonstration in New York in 1924, a clown was employed to caper in front of a slow-moving Model T as it repeatedly rammed him, while the Packard Motor Car Company created and displayed gravestones with the name 'Mr J Walker'. In a performance in Buffalo, an actor was arrested, cuffed, and made to wear a sandwich board labelled, 'I am a jaywalker' before being carted off in a police vehicle covered in anti-pedestrian slogans.[28]

Meanwhile, the National Automobile Chamber of Commerce sought to influence the coverage of traffic fatalities in the media, which had been previously uniformly hostile to drivers. It established itself as a clearing house, curating accounts of fatalities, and offering them, suitably glossed to blame pedestrians, to newspaper editors. The shift in tone was widely noted. 'It is now the fashion to ascribe from 70 to 90 per cent of all accidents to jaywalking,' commented a magistrate in New York City's traffic court.[29]

Today, with cars far more sophisticated than in the past, motor vehicles remain the single leading cause of death for Americans between the ages of four and thirty-four. Convincing the public to accept that toll required a Herculean effort. It would not have been possible without the collapse of other transport options.

Like the Electric Vehicle Company of the 1890s, the streetcar companies were monopolies — and often notoriously corrupt. In many cases, their owners cared little for the service they provided, since their profits came from purchasing real estate on the city fringes and running trolley networks to bump up land prices. As a result, they were often content to sign contracts pledging that, in return for monopoly rights, they would maintain the roads near their rails, and keep fares low. The emerging auto industry could thus attack the old transport barons for unfairly excluding competitors. A streetcar system belonged to a trust, they said, but every American could own a car.

Facing this new competition, the streetcars struggled, locked into paying for the roads on which their new rivals drove. Even a small number of automobiles prevented streetcars from keeping to their schedules, and their unreliability, in turn, encouraged more automobiles.

In Chicago, streetcars retained the right of way — and so managed to survive. But in cities that prioritised cars, the streetcars disappeared. Most famously, in Los Angeles, a consortium consisting of General Motors, Firestone Tire and Rubber Company, Standard Oil, and Phillips Petroleum eventually bought out — and then closed down — that city's streetcar network. The animated film *Who Framed Roger Rabbit?* portrayed the destruction of LA's public transport as an auto conspiracy. But the charge missed the bigger point: street cars, trains, and other public systems required state support that was increasingly devoted to automobiles instead.

Think of Trump's quip about his salt-of-the-earth supporters in Michigan — that family struggling to recharge the electrical vehicle foisted upon them by effete liberals. In 1915, *The New York*

Times noted an auto show displaying a product called the 'electrant', which, it explained to its readers, would 'supply electricity as a hydrant supplies water'. It explained that these devices would soon be 'installed in suburban villages and places on the main lines of travel', with a quarter inserted in the slot sufficient to power a car for twenty-five miles.[30] Had that happened — had an infrastructure of electrants been created — electric vehicles might well have become entirely commonplace, especially since the initial investment would have incentivised constant improvements. But it didn't, and so, as a result, EVs couldn't compete.

It's this failure that permitted Trump to make his gag, confident that, for ordinary Americans, the infrastructural requirements of an electric vehicle seem so quixotic as to sound ridiculous. His listeners didn't recall that the petrol-driven car once faced almost identical problems, which were only solved by state intervention. The modern automobile is a private machine, but one that rests on massive infrastructure built up by public investment over many decades. American drivers today rely upon more than four million miles of roads, almost all of them funded by the taxpayer. The early success of the car thus rested on extraordinary subsidies, without which it probably would not have flourished.[31]

As early as 1924, more than $1 billion had been spent by all levels of government to make roads more suitable for automobiles. By 1939, another $1.4 billion had been allocated. Then, after the Second World War, the industry united with the military-industrial complex to lobby for the 1956 Interstate Highway Act, an allocation of massive federal funding for the national system of interstate and defence highways. It was only on the basis of such support that cars and trucks could become, for the first time, the primary mode of long-haul transport, taking over from the trains that had remained dominant until well into the post-war era. In 1965, some 11.1 million cars rolled off US production lines each year, with one job in six connected to the automobile industry.[32]

The triumph of the car destroyed the cities that had first initially resisted it. In place of the central metropolises in which people lived and worked, the car facilitated the modern suburbs, as population clusters became strung out along an endless highway. Private automobiles allowed Americans to spread, normalising previously unimaginable distances between family members and friends, and separating places of work from places of residence. The sprawling new homes in suburbia provided space for private gadgets and comforts unfeasible in city tenements, with, in a sense, the automobile driving post-war consumer culture.

But if the car enabled people to travel further, it also made that travel mandatory. In a village or a city, one might live surrounded by relatives and friends, with work and leisure close at hand. To make room for cars, distances increased.[33] Greater speeds became possible, but people spent more time travelling, with the car suddenly necessary for the simplest activity: taking children to school, buying bread, visiting parents. The suburbs allowed Americans to acquire more consumer comforts, but they also made those comforts necessary, since in a home physically distant from others, the individual (or individual family) became responsible for feeding, washing, and entertaining themselves in isolation.

Paradoxically, this accounts for the centrality of the car as a signifier of freedom. The freedom trope was heavily pushed by the industry, particularly in opposition to state-backed or centralised modes of transport. 'Americans are a race of independent people,' declared the National Automobile Chamber of Commerce's Roy Chapin. 'Their ancestors came to this country for the sake of freedom and adventure. The automobile satisfies these instincts.'[34]

The independence of the motorist was always illusory. Raymond Williams writes of how, from inside the windowed shell of a car, we experience our trip as the exercise of choice, independence, and free movement. From the side of the road, however, it's obvious that the traffic flow is controlled and regulated by a social order.[35] The pedestrian can travel as he or she sees fit; the equestrian must merely find some grass or oats for his or her horse. The driver, however, requires well-maintained roads, regular servicing, and a constant supply of petrol from stations along the highway.

At the same time, the private car did offer a genuine freedom — but primarily from the conditions that it created. As André Gorz says:

> The car has made the big city uninhabitable. It has made it stinking, noisy, suffocating, dusty, so congested that nobody wants to go out in the evening anymore. Thus, since cars have killed the city, we need faster cars to escape on superhighways to suburbs that are even farther away. What an impeccable circular argument: give us more cars so that we can escape the destruction caused by cars.[36]

The argument might have been circular, but it was compelling nonetheless, with more and more people fleeing to the suburbs. Suburbanisation broke down older urban communities, replacing them with suburbs in which individual families lived autonomous lives, with no necessary relationship with people around them. That gave rise to distinctive ennui, against which Jack Kerouac and the Beats rebelled. Free spirits found solace by taking to the highways, as the car allowed them to escape a suburbanisation created, in part, by the car.

In the 1960s, only 20 per cent of American households ran a second vehicle. Today, that figure tops 65 per cent. Increasingly, Americans are driving alone, with the average occupancy rate slowly sinking.

That's because most working-class people now live significant distances from the suburban rings where jobs are to be found. It's very difficult to find or keep work without driving. Indeed, employers often insist that job applicants have a car, partly because they know that any employee without their own vehicle will struggle with punctuality.

The necessity extends to almost every aspect of life. Buying food — particularly at the big-box stores that offer discounted groceries — means driving, as does visiting a doctor, or going on a holiday, or staying in touch with family.

The relationship between cars and freedom becomes especially clear when we think about those who can't drive. For young people, a car enables an independent social life. If they're old enough to get a licence, they can visit friends, go to gigs, and have sex.

If they're not, they can't.

The same might be said for the elderly. So long as they can drive, it's possible to live in their own homes. As soon as they become too frail to operate a car, they sink into dependency.

Under such circumstances, a stigma around public transport becomes inevitable. Catching a bus feels like a second-class option, a choice only the desperate will make. 'Only one reason buses have such big, wide windows,' says the character played by Ludacris in the 2005 Paul Haggis film *Crash*. 'To humiliate the poor brothers reduced to riding in them.'[37]

The genuine attachment that so many people feel for their cars comes from the same place. Because the first motor vehicles belonged to the rich, driving became an assertion of status for those who weren't wealthy. In any case, as soon as the private car became dominant, every aspect of life was reshaped around it.[38] From the 1920s onwards, as the auto industry changed the country, Americans came to cherish the vehicles that allowed them to do the things that, because of cars, were increasingly impossible without cars.

The working-class parents campaigning against the devastation wreaked by the early cars weren't climate-change activists. Nevertheless, theirs was a struggle over the urban environment, a resistance to the public harms inflicted by private interests. They refused to accept that children should die and that the commons should be privatised simply to facilitate the plans of the automotive industry.

While no one talked about climate change at the dawn of the twentieth century, the pollution created by the automobile was well known. In his 1896 essay making the case for the electric vehicle, Pedro Salom decried the fumes associated with the internal-combustion engine. 'Imagine thousands of such vehicles on the streets,' he wrote, 'each offering up its column of smell ... and consider whether such a system has general utility or adaptability.'[39]

Instead of thousands of such vehicles, we now have more than a billion.

Had the desire of working Americans for safety been prioritised, and their enthusiasm for public space been respected, transport might have been designed on the basis of public good rather than private enrichment. If that had happened, the planet would look very different today.

Instead, a relatively small number of entrepreneurs successfully campaigned to reorganise the country — and subsequently the world — so that their particular business model might succeed.

Denis Leary knows the word for such people.

Still, the triumph of assholedom was not foreordained — and it's worth thinking about what might have been.

CHAPTER TWO

Farewell to Sudan

In 2018, zookeepers in Kenya euthanised the last male northern white rhinoceros.

A widely circulated image shows the animal, known as Sudan, lying on his side with an eye half-closed and one leg tucked under his vast body in a strangely human pose of resignation. The cracks and creases of his hide resemble an ancient mammoth pulled from the tundra, as if mummified already, as if already extinct.

In the photo, Joseph Wachira, a keeper from the Ol Pejeta Conservancy, bids goodbye to the sick and elderly creature, pressing his temple against Sudan's vast forehead. For many, the poignancy of the moment — the last glimpse of the last animal — made an implicit accusation.

You did this. All of you.

Extinctions foster a collective shame, a guilt about belonging to the one species that so unnecessarily exterminates others. Other predators slaughter with abandon, but only so as to feed. The human propensity to extirpate rather than kill marks us as fundamentally different, fundamentally worse.

'For Man is god,' writes the poet Anne Sexton, 'and man is eating the earth up / like a candy bar.'[1]

The lines present humanity's awful power less as numinous than as disgustingly trivial: the sensibility of a greedy child, gorging itself beyond satiety. Fewer than 30,000 rhinos of any species remain alive, but poachers toting automatic weapons and chainsaws still hunt down the survivors. That's because the ground-up horns sell as aphrodisiacs. During his last years in Kenya, Sudan could only graze under an open sky if protected by drones, dogs, and armed guards, all because millionaires paid unimaginable sums for a powder made of keratin — a material that they could obtain from their own fingernails and hair.

'[N]ot one of them can be left alone with the ocean,' Sexton writes, 'for it is known he will gulp it all down.'[2]

A sense of human beings as innately, uniquely destructive corresponds to a particular understanding of the natural kingdom, as defined by a simple opposition. On the one side lies the wilderness, untouched by human hands; on the other, men and women, and all they create. Nature, in this model, signifies the universe without us. Free from human interference, the world simply persists, passive and unchanging — right up until we trample it.

In his influential 1864 book *Man and Nature,* the early ecologist George P Marsh presents the terms of his title as an almost irresolvable contradiction. Writing as European settlers consolidated their hold on America, with the frontier advancing inexorably year by year, Marsh warned that humans would exhaust the land — and more quickly than anyone expected. The riches of the New World were not inexhaustible. Already, old colonists reminisced about the days when migrating ducks darkened the skies, while younger men wondered at their tales of woods swarming with game. Nature, said Marsh, creates a delicate harmony, a gentle music endlessly sustained. To that music, mankind brings only discord, with civilisation's cacophony overpowering melodies of the wild until, eventually, they all fell silent.[3]

While few environmental theorists share Marsh's binary today, for many of us it can seem almost common sense. Unlike his readers, we don't, for the most part, perceive nature as a cornucopia, but rather see deforestation and decline everywhere we look. The environmentalist Bill McKibben describes humanity running Genesis backward, a de-creation that inevitably makes us long for the disappeared. We think of pristine landscapes where Sudan might lumber across untouched plains, tomorrow just as today and yesterday, and the day before. We imagine forests that have never known the axe, crystalline water unsullied by human lips, and mountain peaks, unconquered and proud, stretching high in the distance.

Choked by civilisation, we treasure its opposite.

Environmentalism can, then, mean the protection of nature from its eternal foe, humanity. We value, in particular, areas designated as 'wilderness', places entirely untouched by people. When we can't save the wild, we seek to restore it, undoing, as best we can, the vandalism of the past by erasing prior interventions.

On a day-to-day basis, a simple comparison between the world and the people who live in it works — more or less, most of the time. It provides the vocabulary for outrage when developers bulldoze forests to construct golf courses; it gives moral force to campaigns against climate change.

Yet, on another level, that contrast has always been disastrous. For a start, it presents environmentalism as a doctrine innately detached from ordinary people, the bulk of whom now live in cities. If you inhabit a neighbourhood entirely bounded by concrete and bitumen, a defence of wilderness bears no relation to your day-to-day life. You might admire rainforest gullies and island beaches, but you live under fluorescent lights. What does environmentalism say to you?

More fundamentally, the emphasis on the pristine and the

untouched establishes a program that, almost by definition, cannot succeed. For if we seek a wilderness entirely untainted by humans, we will never find it.

In 2018, researchers examining samples drilled from deep below the Greenland ice sheets made an amazing discovery. The core they studied contained snow that had fallen season after season between 1235 BC and 1257 AD. In those long-buried deposits, frozen time-capsules from the remote past, they found minute particles of lead.[4]

How had that contamination reached the most unspoiled landscape on the planet more than a thousand years ago? In the ancient world, artisans relied on lead for everyday items, from pipes to drinking vessels, so much so that historians estimate the drinking water in early Rome to have been thoroughly toxic. As well as facilitating domestic life, lead played an important role in the production of Roman silver, which was mined and crushed from lead-silver ores, with more lead added before the separation of the metals. The intensity of the forges sent trace emissions high into the atmosphere, where they were picked up on the winds — and blown, eventually, to Greenland.

That pollution deep under ancient ice illustrates an obvious problem with the idea of 'wilderness': namely, land untouched by humanity has always been difficult to find. If by 'wild' we mean 'unaffected by people', wilderness doesn't really exist anywhere — and hasn't for aeons.

As we shall see, the distinction Marsh made between the advance of Man and the retreat of Nature rested on a dismissal of the Native Americans, who had created the landscape he so treasured over thousands of years of firestick farming, hunting, and traditional agriculture. The American wilderness was thus neither primordial nor pristine, but a result of the lives and work of the people who had inhabited it before the Europeans arrived.

The same might be said of the Old World, the land from

which the colonists came. We think of grey squirrels, rabbits, and pheasants as quintessentially English; but, in fact, they're all introduced, while creatures commonplace a thousand years ago — such as beavers, aurochs, cranes, wolves, bears, and boars — have vanished. Conservationists and hikers rightly recognise Britain's ancient woodlands as special places. Yet they often don't realise that the gnarled old trees in them were deliberately planted, and cultivated as sources of timber, fuel, or game. Likewise, readers of *Wuthering Heights* glory in the wild freedom of the North Yorkshire moors, rather than recalling the prosaic labours of foresters who cleared them, tree by tree, during the Bronze and Iron Ages.

New archaeological techniques, from satellite photography to molecular analysis, have enabled scientists to recognise that, as far back as 3,000 years ago, much of the Earth had already been substantially transformed. As researchers Lucas Stephens, Erle Ellis, and Dorian Fuller write:

> [I]t's clearer than ever before that most places we think of as 'pristine' or 'untouched' have long relied on human societies to fill crucial ecological roles. As a consequence, trying to disentangle 'natural' ecosystems from those that people have managed for millennia is becoming less and less realistic, let alone desirable.[5]

In the place of a timeless nature, we need to understand the world's history, both with and without us. Climate change, in particular, forces us to grasp what we've done to the world — but it also makes us cognisant of the immense transformations undergone by the planet long before a certain species of large-brained hominoid came on the scene.

When scientists measure human-induced global heating, they must reconstruct atmospheric and terrestrial developments back into deep time. That means tracing, how, in the course of millennia, temperatures have risen and fallen and risen again, as the Earth cooled and heated and flooded and erupted and endured meteor strikes. For climate researchers, nature appears less a constant state and more the contents of a roiling cauldron, bubbling and hissing and occasionally boiling over. Instead of timeless harmonies, they hear Wagnerian crashes, crescendos, and grand denouements: a music of transformation rather than stasis.

The history of nature shapes the history of humans; the natural world disturbs us just as much as we disturb it. The spread of homo sapiens from Africa seems, for instance, a consequence of climate change, with new patterns of weather dispersing our species from our continent of origin all around the globe. Yet, even when Marsh wrote, his depiction of a simple contrast between an active Man and a passive Nature didn't reflect the extent to which almost every aspect of nineteenth-century American life still depended on ancient cycles. Back then, as throughout most of recorded history, people's daily routines varied with the seasons, tuned to the harvest and the migration of wildlife. A disruption of those rhythms — a frost coming too early or too late; a river flooding or drying up — constituted not an annoyance but an existential threat, a portent of destruction for entire populations.

For we moderns, technology creates an apparent wall between the doings of humans and the workings of nature. We control the temperature with the press of a button, and we soar in aeroplanes high above the trees and rivers. We munch on food that arrives packaged in plastic, and we think ourselves entirely self-sufficient and independent.

Yet the energy that cools us comes from coal, the plane relies on petrol, and our snacks blend potatoes grown in Idaho, oil from processed vegetables, and salt harvested from the sea. Today, just as much as 100,000 years ago, we must eat and drink and shelter and clothe ourselves, activities that depend on our relationship to a world external to us: that is, to nature. Irrespective of the advances of science, our dependence remains, an inevitable consequence of existence for physical, material beings in a physical, material universe. We belong to the nature that we alter.

Humans are not alone in that, of course. Marsh's depiction of a passive and balanced world obscures the changes wrought by other life forms — changes, in some ways, more profound than those we have made. During the first half of the planet's existence, the atmosphere contained no oxygen. We can breathe today only thanks to what scientists identify as the Great Oxidation Event: the result, it seems, of cyanobacteria developing photosynthesis some 2.4 billion years ago and then pumping out vast quantities of waste gases. In other words, living creatures transformed the entire world — and, by doing so, they made possible the proliferation of life that followed.

Similar transformations continue. Rhinos, for instance, create the distinctive savannas on which they depend, digging up the earth with their horns, and fertilising it with their dung.[6]

Their behaviour encourages grass — and then, because they eat only certain plants, they make room for other herbivores. The biodiversity they engender lets gazelles, antelopes, and zebras feed, and thus indirectly sustains major predators. When the rhinoceros herd galumphs to a new area, that area then changes, in ways that alters the ecosystem as a whole.

The famous re-introduction of wolves to Yellowstone National Park in the United States triggered a process known as a trophic cascade, where the wolves reduced the number of elks, which fostered both plants depleted by the elks (willow, cottonwood) as well as bison (with which the elks had competed). A ripple of consequences led, eventually, to a proliferation of grizzly bears and cougars, a result of the intricate, interlaced relationships between flora and fauna.[7]

In some ways, the effect we have on the world can be compared to the influence other species exert. When rhinos forage or wolves hunt, they do so to survive — and their survival depends on interactions with their surrounds. Like those creatures, we must reshape the world in order to live in it. To maintain ourselves, we find food, and secure water, and construct shelter. These activities, which we can describe collectively as labour, alter the environment on which we depend, even as they alter us.

Unlike other creatures, however, humans can make choices about the precise form that alteration takes. We must labour, but we can do so in different ways: we can hunt animals or grow corn; we know how to dig wells as well as quench our thirst in a lake; people can construct a hut — or build a skyscraper. A herd of rhinos remake an African plain, but they do so without conscious decision. There's no rhino architect; the herd doesn't discuss where best to trample. Every bird builds the nest common to its species; every beehive follows a pre-established pattern. Chimpanzees occasionally forage with sticks; some birds drop burning sticks to start fires. But no other species can plan and co-operate and decide what natural resources to use in the manner that humans do.

That defines us as human, and provides the basis of culture. Collective and conscious toil necessitates language — how else might a group work together? The ways we change our world relies on planning and thus abstraction, the thinking that gives rise to mathematics and science. It entails social organisation, methods of co-ordinating a common purpose.

To put it another way, our relationship with nature always means a relationship with other people. When he wrote *Man and Nature*, George P Marsh drew upon his classical education to illustrate the inexorable conflict between humanity and the world. He showed how the Romans, in particular, devastated the environment in ways still visible today. In the territories once occupied by the empire, the modern visitor can see the barrenness on mountain spurs cleared by foresters, with the fields that once fed the Eternal City now unproductive after centuries of overcultivation, erosion, and abuse.[8]

On that basis, Marsh assumed a continuity between ancient and modern times, with thousands of years of environmental degradation simply proving the pernicious effects of humanity. The Romans sent traces of lead up into the atmosphere; we despoil the highest peaks and deepest oceans with microplastics. In the distant past and today, the human race instinctively ruins and degrades.

But let's look again at those frozen particles in Greenland and the story they tell.

The Romans forged so much lead in part because they used it in the empire's currency: a silver coin called the 'denarius'. The necessity of lead to the manufacture of the denarius means that the traces in Greenland can be read as a kind of proxy for the Roman economy. The empire's expansion mandated more coins and more mining, which shows in the snow as more particles, just as years of decline show as less.

The pollution thus chronicles Roman history, thousands of metres below Greenland. The researchers found, for instance, a decrease in particles in ice layers between 108 and 92 BC, a period associated with the disruptive wars Rome fought in Spain. When Julius Caesar became governor of the region, production resumed — and so did pollution. Caesar's assassination in 44 BC, and the brutal civil wars that ensued, showed up in the ice, as did the consolidation of the empire under the Pax Romana from about 27 BC.

The lead provides a remarkable illustration of the relationship between humans and nature, in all its complexity. Like animals, we change the world in order to live. But, unlike animals, we form societies — and those societies shape our interactions with our environment.

We know a little about the conditions prevailing in the Roman mines. The Greek historian Diodorus of Sicily describes an industry of unspeakable brutality, with slaves working day and night deep within the ground, with overseers beating them mercilessly. 'Death in their eyes is more to be desired than life,' Diodorus concludes, 'because of the magnitude of the hardships they must bear.'[9]

The pollution in Greenland came, in other words, from a society deeply divided by class, with a tiny minority exercising power over the bulk of the population. As Rome expanded through imperialist wars, its elite grew fabulously rich from owning silver mines, in which they worked disposable people to death. The slaves creating the lead particles laboured for others. They did not decide how or when they toiled.

The attribution of the particles to 'human nature' means eliding the distinction between the holder of a whip and the person being lashed, in a way that's unjust and historically inaccurate. The lead released by the Romans did not vary according to changes in the human soul, but instead corresponded to relationships between people — in the form of wars, political crises, and the like. The layers of snow show that, even in the ancient world, environmental destruction was the result of particular social pressures, not an unchanging human essence. It was the responsibility of some people, not all people.

The point becomes even clearer in our own time. The fate of the last male northern white rhinoceros offers a warning about the nature of Man — or, at least, it does until you look more closely about how Sudan died and why.

Rhinos and humans coexisted for thousands of years.

The population of the animal began plummeting during the colonial period, a consequence of the Western enthusiasm for big-game hunting. Despite independence, most African countries remain desperately poor. The poachers who systematically kill rhinos today might not be the slaves described by Diodorus, but they're still impoverished, conducting their trade on behalf of the very rich.

Why do the wealthy crave horns? Western journalists usually attribute the black-market demand to the influence of Chinese medicine, claiming that the newly minted millionaires of South-East Asian believe in folk cures for impotence — and will pay anything to get them.

Yet that's not quite true. While traditional healers did, on occasion, prescribe rhino horn, they did not recommend it as an aphrodisiac, but rather for illnesses such as arthritis, gout, fevers, and headaches.[10] The belief that the animals could restore potency developed only in recent times, most probably (and perversely) because of the bogus claims made by Europeans about Chinese cures. The fake journalistic narrative created its own reality, generating the (initially bogus) association it identified between rhinos and sex.

Fundamentally, the desire for horn always stemmed not from its efficacy, but its rarity, with its possession understood as a gesture of conspicuous consumption. Today, the men who dissolve the stuff into expensive alcohol do so instead of taking Viagra or Cialis, because they want to display social power as much as regain sexual potency. The bizarre trade only makes sense in a particular context, one in which the inequality and environmental destruction implicit in powdered horn possesses an almost erotic charge.

But not all civilisations are the same — and not all relate to nature in the same way. Any account of the supposed innate destructiveness of humanity must explain not only those societies that eat up the Earth, but also those that don't.

CHAPTER THREE

The Earth Glows No More Divine

When Europeans arrived in the Americas, genocide ensued — and the deaths of untold millions literally chilled the planet.

That's the conclusion in a paper for *Quaternary Science Reviews*, the result of a project led by Alexander Koch at University College London. He and his team argue that what they call 'The Great Dying' exacerbated the Little Ice Age during which, between about 1570 to the 1680s, global temperatures fell by an average of two degrees Celsius or so.[1]

In that brief and mysterious period, the planet became radically colder. In London, the Thames froze so completely that locals erected a so-called Frost Fair, a semi-permanent entertainment area with wooden huts and even brothels constructed on the iced-over river. Glaciers encroached on the Swiss Alps, vineyards failed in Germany, and the Prussian pastor Daniel Schaller expressed a common sentiment when he concluded that '*ruina mundi* (the ruin of the world) must be at our gates'.[2]

Koch and his colleagues associate the worst of the Little Ice Age with the conquest of the so-called New World, a blood-soaked intervention that unleashed war, slavery, and disease on the native population. The deaths of some 56 million people — 90 per cent of the population in the Americas — disrupted agriculture over more than 50 million hectares, so that forests and jungles grew over land previously used as fields. The trees reasserting themselves in this depopulated landscape absorbed more carbon, reducing the greenhouse effect sufficiently to change global temperatures, with a bleak new climate almost a testament to historic crime.

Koch's thesis remains controversial, not least because the death toll and the acreage of indigenous agriculture rests on uncertain estimates. Nevertheless, his argument illustrates, in the grimmest fashion, a broader point. The New World celebrated by explorers was never the wilderness they imagined. On the contrary, the 'pristine' landscape that the first Westerners encountered marked a very human history, on a continent changed by its original inhabitants over thousands of years.

The continent of Australia provides a particularly striking example of the same phenomenon, since its Indigenous people had maintained a culture stretching back into deep time. Yet when Captain James Cook stared out over the land, he declared his 'discovery' to be 'in the pure state of Nature, the Industry of Man [having] had nothing to do with any part of it'.[3] In reality, the industry of man had everything to do with the places that Cook most valued. Indigenous people in Australia did not live in a 'state of Nature' — or, at least, not in any simple way. Like the peoples of the Americas and elsewhere, they shaped, through their labour, the environment on which they depended. The fate of that environment explains a great deal about climate change today.

In 1770, Cook wrote of the east coast of Australia as being so clear that 'the whole country or at least a great part of it might be cultivated without being obliged to cut down a single tree'. Sydney Parkinson, a draughtsman and painter on Cook's expedition, concurred, calling the land 'pleasant and fertile', and describing the trees as 'like plantations in a gentleman's park'.[4] The similes they used reveal more than either man understood. The terrain the explorers so admired had, in fact, been created by Indigenous people to foster game animals — precisely as British aristocrats used their private estates or parks as hunting grounds.

All across the continent, Indigenous people lit fires to thin the bush, fertilise the soil, and encourage the grasses preferred by the animals they hunted. The historian Bill Gammage argues that they developed a complicated methodology resting on what he calls 'templates': particular associations of disparate plant species, maintained over decades or even centuries. They selected a notable topographic feature — such as a lake, a mountain, or a rock — and then reshaped the surrounds to complement it, alternating varieties of vegetations to create effects that suited them and the game they sought.[5]

The template system depended on a sophisticated knowledge of animals and plants, a theology that mandated protocols for tending the land, with particular groups responsible for maintaining the areas with which they were associated. Taboos and other cultural prohibitions discouraged the taking of plants and animals in circumstances that might diminish the long-term viability of species; similar obligations ensured that burns were performed only when and where they were required.

The method did more than sustain the population. It generated abundance, and did so efficiently: Indigenous people seem to have spent no more than three or four hours each day seeking food.[6] While nourishing the human population, the templates fostered ecological diversity, and so confounded the usual perception of people as innately ruinous. In pre-capitalist Australia, humans did not despoil the land. They consciously and deliberately improved it. Rather than silencing nature, they harmonised with plants and animals in a richer and more intricate music.

In a letter from south-western Victoria, the settler John G Robertson explained to lieutenant-governor Charles La Trobe about how, immediately after settlement, he'd witnessed the herbaceous plants disappear from what had previously been lush pasture, with the silk grass growing more and more extensively and displacing the annuals that had once held the soil together. The colonists could only watch helplessly as land that they had thought inexhaustibly fertile became barren clay, exposed to the sun, and eroded in all directions.[7]

Catastrophic transformations of this sort took place all around the first Europeans, with the old gentlemen's parks disintegrating literally under their feet. The persistent resistance to colonisation by the traditional owners reflected their awareness of the destruction taking place. In Port Phillip, after only four years of white settlement, the land had become so damaged and depleted that it could no longer produce the food on which Indigenous people relied. The missionary Joseph Orton recorded a native population that had previously known only abundance teetering on the brink of starvation, surviving only by begging for introduced supplies.[8]

It's important to understand what this meant.

Orton wasn't witnessing the despoliation of an Eden, nor experiencing the inevitable consequences of humans trespassing on wilderness. On the contrary, the new desolation owed less to people's presence than it did to their absence, with the settlers dispersing the Indigenous inhabitants who fought desperately to maintain the local ecology. Once again, the devastation could not be attributed to humanity as a species, since some people mounted a life-and-death struggle against the acts carried out by others.

The colonists brought with them herds of domestic animals (predominantly sheep and cattle), and these creatures' hooves — radically different from the pads of native species — systematically uprooted the native grasslands. Even more importantly, the settlers introduced a concept of land ownership incompatible with the practices of the locals. The white people could not and would not allow the burning that had been performed since ancient times, seeing fire as an intolerable imposition on private property and as a threat to domesticated animals, which could not disperse to escape flames as kangaroos and most other native species did. The introduction of European agriculture — backed up with European guns — meant that land assiduously maintained over thousands of years was depleted at a remarkable speed, with the grasses vanishing so completely that today we scarcely recall their existence.[9]

The unmaking of the continent resulted not from human activity so much as the wrong kind of human activity. After all, the colonists were initially a minority, and probably did not outnumber the diminished Indigenous population until the mid-1840s — and, as late as 1850, the total population in Australia was probably still 25 per cent smaller than the total population prior to colonisation.[10] The heartbreaking erosion witnessed by Robertson and so many others could not be attributed to overpopulation. Instead, a relatively tiny number of Europeans prevented a larger number (at least at first) of Indigenous people from maintaining the environment in the way that they'd done for tens of thousands of years.

In a pre-capitalist Indigenous society, the population used land to produce food and other resources for direct needs, with trade only a minor and distinctly secondary consideration. Of necessity, the people integrated human labour into natural, local cycles, ensuring that the soil in a particular area remained fertile, with the plants propagated and the animal populations robust.

Even though Indigenous communities practised agriculture, they harvested only what they could carry, and so their crops did not generate the surplus that might support any section of the community in idleness. The material basis for a separate ruling caste of priests or administrators did not exist; all contributed to a production from which all benefited directly. The early anthropologist WEH Stanner concluded that traditional society lacked substantive property inequality and any kind of class division, with master-servant relationships unknown among the people he studied.[11]

That equality, and the social stability it brought, facilitated the system of collective land management. In Roman society, an elite directed production for their own enrichment; in Indigenous Australia, labour necessarily involved the consent of all. The academic Fred Myers described how, among the Pintupi people of the Central Desert, no one possessed an authority that legitimated automatic command over others, and so decisions resulted from protracted negotiation.[12]

This egalitarianism was common among pre-class societies. Eleanor Burke Leacock's classic account of the Naskapi of Canada notes their society's emphasis on group decisions, on consensus, 'on generosity, on co-operation, on patience and good humour'.[13] Such values minimised the ruination of resources for private gain because it encouraged individuals to work for collective prosperity. Culture, religion, and custom reinforced the sentiment, mandating behaviour that renewed the land, and prohibiting conduct that depleted necessary resources.

The Europeans who arrived in Australia after 1788 lived very differently. Though planned as a militarised penal colony, the occupation quickly established capitalist social relations on new soil.[14] This meant a society based on the generalised exchange of commodities: products of human labour that, while useful, are made to be exchanged, rather than to satisfy an immediate need. Having travelled immense distances under perilous conditions, pastoralists sought to make as much money as they could, as quickly as they could.[15] They weren't raising sheep because they wanted wool; they were creating items for sale — and as many of them as possible. By

1829, some half a million sheep were being grazed in the colony; wool exports rose from a value of £34,900 in 1830 to £566,100 in 1840.[16]

If capitalists shared the Roman proprietors' interest in money, they were, at base, driven by imperatives quite different from those prevailing in the ancient civilisations. The integration of the colonial agricultural industry into a global economy had profound consequences for the relationship between people and nature. The settlers saw themselves as 'improving' the land, but not in any way that would have made sense to its original owners. The market demanded cattle, sheep, and other familiar products, rather than the kangaroos and grasses harvested by Indigenous people. As the ecologist Richard Levins quips, capitalist agriculture produces profit, with food a mere side effect — and, in the Australian context, profit mandated innately destructive practices.[17]

Competition meant that landowners could never simply enrich themselves and be done. It was not feasible for them to stockpile their money and then live like emperors, indifferent to further gains. They needed returns on their investments, not once but again and again. Each landowner faced the same pressure to reinvest profits, to grow and to innovate, knowing that if they didn't, they would be unable to compete with their rivals.

The drive to accumulate gave British settlement its expansionary dynamic, with new arrivals quickly spreading across the best land. Even if the European landowners had comprehended Indigenous practices for tending the soil, they could not have implemented them. The patient rituals that sustained humans for aeons on the continent could not be performed because of the very specific priorities baked into the new system. An individual pastoralist might mourn the disappearance of lush fields and green pastures, but his private sentimentality bore no relationship to his business. Even if he recognised the superior wisdom of Indigenous agriculturists, it meant nothing to him, since he was impelled by a market with its own distinct and different requirements.

The arrival of capitalism didn't merely change the relationship with the land; it changed the relationship between people. In pre-capitalist society, people worked, but not according to the dictates of wage labour. As a settler in New South Wales pointed out in the 1830s, 'they are not labourers at all, and for the same reason that any other gentleman is not [namely] that he can live without labour'.[18] By this, he did not mean they were idle, but simply that nothing forced them to go into others' employ: like English gentlemen on their estates, they could decide for themselves what they did, how they did it, and for what purpose.

By contrast, capitalism — as a system of universalised commodity production — treated the human ability to work as just another commodity. The agricultural businessmen settling the country needed to buy labour power. They needed a class that they could employ with wages.

Today, we take the wages system for granted. It appears normal, almost eternal, since we can barely conceive of an alternative. It did not seem normal to pre-colonial people. In Australia, as elsewhere in the world, they found capitalist practices utterly horrifying.

The commodification of labour means that once employers buy our labour power, it belongs to them for a certain time. During the working day, they determine what we do. Of necessity, they demand relentless concentration on the tasks they set for us. If they don't wring the maximum productivity from our labour, their business falls behind that of their more ruthless rivals.

Indigenous people, accustomed to an egalitarian ethos and to work carried out for the collective good, saw the authority exerted by employers as tyranny. As late as 1888, a churchman complained of the difficulty he had in persuading Indigenous people that one man was innately better than another, that a certain individual, by virtue of his possessions, mandated obedience from his fellows.[19]

Historian Henry Reynolds provides a long list of complaints from Europeans about the indifference to wages by local people who simply saw no reason to labour in the style of, and with the intensity demanded by, capitalists. They would, occasionally, work for the settlers; but when they did so, they understood themselves as performing a favour, a sentiment that they often conveyed to their appalled masters. Even if they were paid, they arrived when they chose, and they left when they wanted, doing the tasks important to them and disdaining others.[20]

The problem was neither one of stamina nor of aptitude, but rather pertained directly to their relationship with nature. Accustomed to taking with little difficulty food and other resources from the wild storehouse they'd constructed all around them, they could not recognise any justification for the patterns of work that the Europeans required. In Western Australia, the protector of Aborigines noted that Indigenous people did not see the necessity of labouring for colonists, because they preferred the 'precarious subsistence' of the bush and saw their 'roving life' as superior to the 'habits and customs of civilization'.[21] He was correct, except insofar as he regarded their subsistence as 'precarious': prior to 1788, the standard of living for Indigenous people seems to have been considerably higher than most of the English working class. (James Boyce notes how, in the early years of Van Diemen's Land, many convicts simply slipped away to enjoy, like Indigenous people, 'a life of quiet freedom in the well-watered, game-rich bush'.)[22]

But that wasn't the main point. Indigenous people did not despise wage labour primarily because of the effort that it entailed. Rather, they thought the work demanded by capitalists stripped life of its humanity. In 1849, a Victorian justice of the peace identified the issue, explaining that Indigenous men and women looked at shepherds, hutkeepers, bullock drivers, splitters, and other employers as people condemned to a single tedious task. They could not comprehend why anyone would accept such monotony, such empty, soulless drudgery, when the bush itself provided the basis for a life of material satisfaction and spiritual enrichment.[23]

By definition, wage labourers did not work for any purpose that mattered to them. They sold their ability to labour to someone else, and toiled as directed. The commodification of labour power meant that, in principle, any person was replaceable by any other person, just as any job could be substituted for another. As a result, workers on pastoral or agricultural businesses possessed no necessary connection to their task, to their workmates, or to the land.

When Indigenous people gathered food, or burned the bush, or fulfilled other customary tasks, they provided food, clothing, and shelter for themselves and those around them, not for a boss or for a distant customer. They were not impelled by an abstraction like money; they were meeting the immediate obligations of necessity, in ways hallowed by tradition and exulted by theology. Their labour — hunting, burning the bush, sowing and collecting plants — combined what the Europeans would describe as work, recreation, worship, art, and much else besides. Daily tasks were not separate from other aspects of life, but were integrated into them, in a manner that the wages system simply couldn't allow.

The environmental damage of white settlement was not the inevitable result of human activity, but the consequence of a particular sort of human activity, one that Indigenous people did their best to resist. European observers tended to explain the Indigenous hostility to wage labour as a product of race or culture. Yet the Australian colony itself provides striking evidence to the contrary, simply because it came into being — at least in part — in response to a very similar transformation within England itself.

Until the early modern period, many people in rural Europe also depended on collective, non-capitalist practices for their day-today survival — practices that they, too, saw as giving life meaning and value. Feudalism was, of course, a very different system from that which prevailed in Australia, not least because it mandated a tremendous disparity between the privileged aristocracy and people who possessed neither wealth nor power. But, unlike the capitalism that replaced it, the feudal order recognised reciprocal rights and obligations, including those customs through which peasants collectively tended various natural resources to sustain a community.

Many of England's poorest relied on the so-called commons: shared lands in which they grazed cattle, collected fruits and berries, and perhaps raised some crops. The management of such areas depended on a social world of rituals, feasts, and festivals, structures through which the folk made sense of their often-difficult lives.

Ordinary people did not own much, and many lived in something close to destitution. But they leavened their poverty with regular feasts, celebrations, and religious spectacles, with some estimates suggesting that, in pre-capitalist northern Europe, most of the population devoted about one-third of their working days engaged in activities other than labour.[24] That folk culture mandated a way of living far more attuned to the natural cycles than what was to come.

The development of capitalism first disrupted and then destroyed these older traditions. Throughout the fifteenth and sixteenth centuries, feudal landowners realised they could make fortunes growing wool for the textile industry, and so they forcibly enclosed vast tracts of land previously held in common. The population resisted desperately, with the enclosures spurring years of petitions, protests, and riots. 'Here we were we born and here we will die,' people in Dorset announced as they repelled the local sheriff.[25] Nevertheless, the successful transformation of shared land into private property forced huge numbers into near starvation. Surveying the human consequences, Thomas More commented sarcastically that 'sheep ... have become so greedy and fierce that they devour men themselves. They devastate and depopulate fields, houses and towns.'[26] A subsequent round of clearances took place in the late eighteenth century — this time pertaining to the embrace of grain. By 1840, a country that had once been mostly open was almost entirely enclosed.[27] The customary systems of land management gave way to an agricultural capitalism that treated the soil merely as a source of profit.

Unable to survive in the old ways, displaced people straggled into the cities, whose markets and industry grew on the back of destructive rural 'improvement'. Like the Indigenous men and women uprooted by white settlement in Australia, many of those who could no longer live on the land resorted to begging — and, in some cases, to criminality.[28] The British state responded with viciously punitive legislation, including the Riot Act of 1715 (banning public disturbances); the Combination Act of 1721 (outlawing the forerunners of unions); the Workhouse Act of 1723 (under which the poor could be set to compulsory labour); the Black Act of 1723 (providing death sentences for poaching game or collecting wood); and the Vagrancy Act of 1744 (which made lacking employment a crime). Between 1688 and 1820, the number of offences attracting the death penalty increased from fifty to over 220.[29]

Looking back from 1857, an appalled Charles Phillips wrote, 'Every page of our statute book smelt of blood.'[30]

Yet bloodshed was only part of the transformation imposed by the English elite on the mass of the population. Alongside executions, torture, and imprisonment, the authorities also dealt with the swelling criminal class through transportation — including to the new colony in Botany Bay.

By a grotesque irony, the dispossession of Indigenous people in Australia can be traced to a similar dispossession in England itself, with the settlement of the new country, driven, at least, in part, by the need to rebuild a different order in the old one.[31] Some 70 per cent of the Irish convicts and 59 per cent of the English transported to Botany Bay were first-time offenders, most commonly convicted of petty theft: a record that hints at criminality fostered by the complete destruction of an older way of life.[32]

By forcing the rural poor out of their traditional villages, the enclosures created a social layer with no choice but wage labour. The workforce of the English Industrial Revolution came into being through an implicit violence not unlike that unleashed in Australia, as the indigent bid farewell to their land and ventured into the factory, less through any enthusiasm than because of a compulsion backed ultimately by force.[33] People who previously would have fed and clothed themselves by their own labour suddenly no longer could, as, even in the countryside, capitalism prevailed.

That experience was, again, utterly wrenching. The new regime meant that people worked far harder than would have been imaginable previously. In 1200, an adult male in England might have laboured for an estimated 1,620 hours per year; by 1840, the figure stood as high as 3,588.[34]

Even more significantly, artisans or peasants displaced from their ancestral communities and into the cities were inducted into an entirely new culture. The old ways were intimate and personal, based on specific obligations to individual people, and resting upon a profound relationship with the land, forged over the generations. Suddenly, the face-to-face economy of the pre-capitalist order gave way to the impersonality of commodity exchange, with villagers no longer striving for purposes transparent to them, but instead reduced to cogs in much larger industrial machines, the priorities of which remained largely mysterious. Instead of planning their hours according to the rising of the sun and the cycles of the season, they confronted an abstract time that began and ended with shrill factory whistles.[35]

Before the industrial system could function properly, the owners needed to normalise conduct markedly at odds with the values most people cherished. The new proletarians had to arrive punctually (rather than sleeping in, if, say, they were hung over); to perform precisely the task needed (and never do anything else); to keep quiet during work hours (rather than chatting, singing, swearing, or arguing); to maintain a regular output instead of working in bursts; and to think of nothing but the repetitive duties assigned to them. They had to accept that this new method of labour would occupy far more of their time than had previously been allocated to work, and they had to discard, as obstacles to progress, the traditional habits and customs by which they'd made sense of their lives and tended their country.[36]

The rhetoric of the early English manufacturers about their employees thus replicates, almost exactly, the attitude of colonialist employers to Indigenous people. They complained, for instance, that their workforce was transient, insubordinate, and unreliable. The factory owner Samuel Greg Junior vented about the 'restless and migratory spirit' of factory hands; the entrepreneur Thomas Arkwright bemoaned the difficulty in training staff 'to renounce their desultory habits of work'.[37]

In Australia, both governor Macquarie and governor Gipps formulated strategies by which Indigenous people could be broken from what the former called their 'wild wandering and unsettled habits' and induced, as Gipps put it, be 'to become voluntary labourers for wages'.[38] In Perth, the government decreed that Indigenous people could only enter town if they were wearing a woollen shirt earned through labour — a dictate specifically intended to convey a lesson about the value of property. Religion played a key role: the assistant protector of Aborigines, Edward Stone Parker, declared 'the permanent civilisation of the savage is dependent on the influence of Christian instruction'.[39] Other settlers swore by early education, with one official in Western Australia advocating, in 1840, a scheme to remove children from their parents and raise them in institutions that would school them in wage labour.[40]

Such schemes reprised methods used to discipline the working class back in Europe. In the late eighteenth century, industrialists complained that the 'common people' near Edinburgh would do 'very little for wages' and refused to 'exert themselves farther than what they deem necessaries'.[41] In a revealing metaphor, mill managers described the experience of subjecting the locals to the long confinement of the factory as 'like putting a deer in the plough', almost as if, in harnessing the populace to the wage system, they were domesticating nature itself.[42]

As in Australia, religion facilitated the required socialisation, with employers funding churches, chapels, and Sunday Schools in every village and town centre, on the basis that ministers preached a gospel of obedience. As in Australia, children were believed more susceptible than their parents, with the philosopher John Locke opining they could begin work from the age of three. In Norwich, the novelist Daniel Defoe noted with approval that infants aged four or five were held responsible for earning their own bread, though an employer at the Catrine cotton mills admitted that the children he employed were 'very much beat at first before they could be taught their business'.[43]

In both Australia and England, the acceptance of wage labour came from the destruction of other options. In both countries, the old order was shattered, in part by physical violence, since the new regime ultimately relied on soldiers with guns. Expelled from their lands and thus unable to feed and shelter themselves in their customary manner, people either accepted capitalist discipline, or else became entirely destitute.

We're accustomed to acknowledge the relationship between Indigenous society and the land, a relationship that enabled human beings to sustainably manage an immense continent over a vast time.

But, even in feudal England, ordinary people valued their direct engagement with nature, too, and mourned deeply its destruction. John Clare, the poet of the enclosures, explained:

Each little tyrant with his little sign.
Shows where man claims, earth glows no more divine.[44]

For Clare, closer than us to the transition between social orders, capitalism disenchanted the land, profaning the previously sacred ritual by which people had once related to their environment. New priorities were forced, painfully and brutally, on the bulk of the population, in ways that made environmental stewardship impossible and facilitated the crisis we now face.

Some scholars now date the onset of the Anthropocene — the age in which human activity became the defining factor in planetary change — to the destruction of Indigenous societies, precisely because the introduction of a different economic logic so fundamentally changed the human attitude to nature.[45] The conquest of the Americas, in particular, exacerbated an ice age — and then, slowly, began to heat the world.

Today, as the temperatures vault year upon year, we can easily think of humanity as fundamentally hostile to nature. Yet, in historical terms, we've only lived as we do now for the merest blink of an eye. Compared to the cultures they displaced, the settler states are shockingly recent. In one sense, that makes the damage they've done more appalling. But it also provides the basis for hope.

For 50,000 years, Indigenous Australians enhanced the land on which they lived. Their example, and that of other native peoples, shows an ecological society to be possible, and not some kind of dream or utopia. It is the devastation wrought since 1788 that is anomalous, not the tens of thousands of years of stewardship that preceded it.

CHAPTER FOUR

The Water Wheel and the Iron Man

'I became myself capable of bestowing animation upon lifeless matter!' boasts Victor Frankenstein in Mary Shelley's great gothic novel, *Frankenstein*.[1] Shelley's book — subtitled *the modern Prometheus* — emerged from an era of tremendous upheaval, and so provides a useful framework for understanding how capitalism reshaped the human attitude to nature.

In the book, the scientist Victor Frankenstein constructs his creature from parts taken from 'charnel houses', and then animates them through the application of 'galvanic force', or electricity. In those scenes, Shelley drew upon several widely publicised real-life experiments. A few decades earlier, Luigi Galvani had shown that electric currents would cause newly dead frogs to twitch and kick; his nephew, Giovanni Aldini, extended the principle by shocking human corpses.[2]

An even more sensational example of galvanic reanimation took place in 1818 — the same year that *Frankenstein* appeared. In a paper for the Glasgow Literary Society entitled 'An account of some Experiments made on the Body of a Criminal immediately after Execution, with Physiological and Practical Observations', a certain professor Andrew Ure explained how he had attached his 'philosophical apparatus' (basically, a large battery) to the partially disassembled cadaver of an executed murderer by the name of Matthew Clydesdale.[3]

'[F]ifty shocks, each greater than the preceding one, were given in two seconds,' Ure wrote, '[and] every muscle in his countenance was simultaneously thrown into fearful action; rage, horror, despair, anguish, and ghastly smiles …'[4]

It was, he concluded, a display far surpassing any performance by the greatest actors of the day, one that so alarmed the spectators in the gallery that a gentleman fainted and several others fled, nauseated or in horror. When, upon the further application of the apparatus, Clydesdale's arm extended convulsively, many briefly believed the dead man had been re-animated.

The dissections that inspired Shelley reflected a sudden popularity of science among respectable society. In the early-modern period, European gentlemen scientists embraced a fashion for anatomy — so much so that, in the eighteenth century, men of leisure occasionally equipped their residences with private dissecting rooms.[5] The interest was very much a project of the ruling caste, not merely because anatomists were often associated with developing industries, but also because the bodies they cut and probed and dissected invariably came from the poor.

In London, for instance, the town council legislated that dead paupers could be claimed for anatomy. Yet a persistent shortage of cadavers meant that body snatchers (known as 'resurrectionists' or 'sack-em-up men') could make a good living by digging up and selling the freshly deceased, forcing the bereaved to keep guard on tombs or encase the dead in metal.

The rise of a so-called corpse economy echoed broader developments in the way that men and women related to each other. As a system of general commodity exchange, capitalism relied on the buying and selling of everything, including human labour power. If something so fundamental to humanity could be purchased, why should the dead be exempt?

Corpses duly became sought-after items, measured and sold by the inch or by weight in an intricate trade in which human meat could be packed into boxes, roped like hams, stored in barrels, or salted for preservation. When no longer fresh enough for dissection, body parts were simply discarded: incinerated, interred in unmarked graves, or, on occasion, used for dog food.[6]

Inevitably, some resurrection men drew the obvious conclusion from the relative worth of the dead versus the living. William Burke and William Hare, for instance, murdered at least sixteen people in the late 1820s so that their bodies could be sold to the anatomist Dr Robert Knox. A Glasgow street rhyme of the 1820s recorded their relationship thus: 'Burke's the butcher, Hare's the thief/Knox the boy that buys the beef'.[7] When Victor Frankenstein refers in passing to 'the horrors' of his 'secret toils' in 'the unhallowed damps of the grave', readers would have understood precisely what was meant.

The 1752 Murder Act sought to undercut the corpse economy by stipulating that, after execution, the condemned could be dissected (rather than gibbeted in chains), thus providing anatomists with a legitimate source of bodies. Clydesdale, for instance, arrived on Ure's slab because, after imposing a capital sentence, the Glasgow court had also stipulated dissection (a fate later met by both Burke and Hare).

Such sentences were intended to be punitive as much as scientific, with the statute describing the treatment awaiting a murderer as 'a further Terror and peculiar Mark of Infamy'.[8] The perceived need for a punishment more extreme than death itself reflected the uncertainty of a tumultuous age. Whereas the initial enclosures led to an increase in criminality and vagabondage, the development of the new regime eventually spurred more direct resistance. Shelley wrote her novel in the wake of the Luddite revolts, an early working-class rebellion against the new industrial order. As she revised the book in 1817, executions of Luddite leaders were still taking place. A few years later, Scottish weavers led an insurrection calling upon their fellow workers 'to desist from their labour from and after this day ... and attend wholly to the recovery of their Rights'. Their revolt was crushed; its leaders (all weavers) were publicly executed and then ritually dismembered.[9]

In his literary presentation,[10] Ure described Clydesdale — who had worked in textile factories — as a 'middle sized, athletic and extremely muscular man, about thirty years of age', an assessment in which we can perhaps detect a note of class fear. Yet that anxiety made the experiment more significant. With his 'philosophical apparatus', Ure discovered he could, at least briefly, control Clydesdale's muscular frame, making, as he said, the dead fingers move as nimbly as those of a violin performer. In the context of a working-class insurgency, this mysterious power — a gentleman bending a weaver to his will — took on an obvious significance.

Yet, after a few shudders, Clydesdale's corpse subsided. Unlike in Shelley's novel, real galvanisation produced no continuing animation. It took professor Ure another seventeen years to find a lasting alternative, one that he eventually expounded on in an influential book entitled *The Philosophy of Manufactures*.

Today, we'd classify Ure's text as management theory, an early instance of a now-ubiquitous genre. Throughout *The Philosophy of Manufactures*, the professor celebrates the scientific achievements of his day, an era of extraordinary technological progress. In 1763, James Watt unveiled the first practical steam engine; in 1770, James Hargreaves patented the 'Spinning Jenny' engine for working with wool or cotton; in 1804, Richard Trevithick sent a viable steam locomotive chugging down a track. Everywhere, entrepreneurial mechanics tinkered with new gadgets and industrial techniques.

Such innovation grew from capitalism's inner logic. In earlier societies, discoveries unveiled by particular inventors might not necessarily pass into widespread use, simply because previous social structures did not require the constant increases in productivity mandated by capitalism. The tools on which Indigenous people depended had been perfected over thousands of years, to suit the needs of their users. But by the late eighteenth and early nineteenth century, each industrialist assiduously noted improvements made by rivals, and then did his best to trump them — for if he didn't, he would go broke. Advances quickly became generalised; new machines spread throughout industries and, eventually, the economy as a whole.

In a sense, the high-tech world in which we now live assembled itself in the early years of the nineteenth century, with Ure sounding like a modern Silicon Valley entrepreneur spruiking technical progress. The innovations freed the workman, he said, from exhausting his mind, fatiguing his eyes, or wearing out himself through repetitions. Industrial machines were, in fact, 'philanthropic', a testament to the fundamental 'humanity of science'.

In one place, the professor describes children spinning textiles, and can't help but marvel at their good fortune to be so gainfully employed.

'The work of these lively elves resembled a sport,' he exclaims.[11]

Obviously, that bore no relationship to the truth — most visitors to factories confirmed the remarks of a magistrate from 1819 about how remarkably 'puny and squalid' the underage employees were.[12]

Like many IT writers today, Ure thus conflated the potential of science with its function. In a different society, the increased productivity facilitated by machines might, indeed, have reduced the toll that textile production took on weavers, offering them more control over their labour by which they shaped the world, helping them create beautiful work for purposes that made sense to them.

But in the nineteenth century, machines served a quite different purpose. The factory did not spare workers from painful repetition, but instead made that repetition more difficult to avoid.

Ure focused on children because, as he acknowledged elsewhere, few people over the age of puberty could actually bear factory labour. For the most part, those who entered the workshop as adults could not overcome what Ure called 'their listless or restive habits', and so either resigned or were sacked. As a result, maintaining labour discipline was, he admitted, 'a Herculean enterprise'.[13]

There was no mystery as to why.

In the pre-capitalist world, artisans mastered, over a long period, every element of their craft. The apprentice blacksmith learned how to tend the forge and read its colours; how to assess metals; how to swing the hammer; how to draw down iron and shrink it, and bend it and punch it; and a myriad of other techniques. Creating objects for use rather than exchange, artisanal workers began and finished each job, overseeing the task from conception to conclusion. An artisan took pride in her work, aware of the beauty and the value of the pieces that she constructed, and their importance to the community: in a sense, she created works of art as much as items of utility.

The first capitalists had based their ventures on this already-established artisanal culture. The textile industry, in particular, depended on craft knowledge — and that meant skilled workers exerted considerable influence on how and at what pace work was performed. They could demand decent wages, confident that the employers needed their talents; they could find at least some satisfaction in the work they understood better than their bosses.

Employers soon chafed at the independence shown by weavers and other skilled labourers, an independence that ran counter to the logic of commodified labour power. Under the feudal system, a lord ordered a peasant to deliver a specific and concrete outcome, such as the tilling of a particular field. Capitalism, however, rested on the exchange of commodities, with the sale of labour power no different from any other purchase. Once the capitalist paid wages, he 'owned' labour power — and thus felt entitled to direct his employees over the time for which he'd paid.

Competition turned that right into an obligation, since those capitalists who didn't make their labourers toil at maximum efficiency lost out to the capitalists who did. The factory owner obsessing about the technology used by other proprietors also compared his outputs and inputs to theirs, and needed methods to make his employees work precisely as directed.

That was what Ure's book provided.

As the Industrial Revolution developed, employers recognised that, by breaking craft skills into component pieces, they could prevent labourers from cloaking their activities in the mysteries of their guild. They could reduce their wage bills by employing unskilled workers who would also be more pliable than artisans confident in their own talents. Factories began to implement a more and more extreme division of labour, hiring workers to perform a simple, repetitive task rather than to complete an entire job. New workers no longer learned a trade, but were schooled in the specific duty that a workplace required of them, in a way that destroyed their control over their work and increased the control of their managers.

Both sides understood the stakes. The Luddite rebels, for instance, campaigned to defend skilled work in textiles, conscious that its destruction would erode wages and conditions more generally. From the opposite perspective, professor Ure presented his management principles as a means by which employers might use the 'resources of science' to maintain themselves 'in their legitimate rule (sic), that of the head over the inferior members'.[14]

As his book progresses, the airy rhetoric about philanthropy gives way to a cold consideration of technology as a weapon. He explains the factory system as a method to partition manufacture into its essential components, based upon the division of labour among artisans — and asserts that the substitution of machinery for hand skill makes that division much easier to maintain.

'When capital enlists science into her service,' Ure declares, 'the refractory hand of labour will always be taught docility'.[15]

The most modern facilities, designed around huge spinning wheels and wheezing boilers, allowed an engine to allocate, through its various gears, levers, and pulleys, the specific tasks performed by humans. The men no longer obeyed a human head, but rather followed the dictates of a mechanical brain, one for whom mortal thoughts and desires mattered not at all.

For industrialists, this was the breakthrough that science provided: it eroded the power of skilled workers through machines that replicated their talents and set the pace for the entire factory. Technology gave the manager tremendous authority over how the men worked, an authority even more absolute because it was delegated to their mechanical servants. The more the workers lost their agency, the more the factory came alive — becoming, as Ure puts it, a 'vast automaton, composed of various mechanical and intellectual organs, acting in an uninterrupted concert for the production of a common object, all of them being subordinated to a self-regulating moving force'.[16]

It's a passage that recalls his ghastly experiments with Clydesdale's corpse, depicting an entire workforce as if re-animated by galvanism.

He praises, in particular, the so-called self-acting mule designed by Richard Roberts, a contraption that rendered superfluous the skilled craftsman who had previously kept the spinning process in motion. The device — popularly nicknamed 'the Iron Man' — replaced his efforts with a relentless mechanical motion that never slackened nor yielded to any entreaties to slow down.

Ure describes the Iron Man as 'the modern Prometheus', echoing the subtitle of Mary Shelley's novel. But where Dr Frankenstein created a monster from re-animated flesh, the professor celebrates one powered by steam — a 'machine apparently instinct with … thought, feeling and tact' — and dedicated to the restoration of order among the industrious classes. Frankenstein's creation might have choked his wife, Elizabeth, but Ure possesses no doubt as to where the Iron Man's repressive potential will be directed. News about the machine, he gloats, dismayed would-be unionists, and so, 'even long before it left its cradle, so to speak, it strangled the Hydra of misrule'.[17]

The Iron Man demonstrated why technology did not constitute a 'blessing' to most of the population. Factory machines were not implemented to free the workman from his toil, but rather to do the opposite. As Ure stresses, the 'new mechanical tactics' meant that labourers who didn't do as instructed 'found their flanks turned and their defences rendered useless … and were obliged to surrender at discretion'.[18]

The weaponisation of machinery explains the extraordinary environmental destruction unleashed during this time. As Britain's factories embraced what Ure calls 'the benignant power of steam', the Industrial Revolution required ever-greater quantities of coal — and coal served as a gateway to other forms of fossil energy. If the nineteenth century foreshadowed our technological present, it also set in train our ecological catastrophe.

But it did not have to be that way.

Steam's importance to the Industrial Revolution can imply that humanity embraced coal — and fossil fuels as a whole — as the price for scientific advancement. But that narrative does not fit with the facts. As Andreas Malm demonstrates in his magisterial *Fossil Capital*, the textile business — the original locus of the Industrial

Revolution — began with renewable energy. Industrialists such as Richard Arkwright built their empires with mills located on rivers, using running water to grind their mills — a technique known since Roman times, and one that remained dominant in British industry well into the 1830s.[19]

The factory system's early reliance on hydropower rather than coal might be dismissed as the temporary embrace of a transitional energy, one inevitably abandoned as industry advanced. Yet though industrialists did, eventually, shift to fossil energy, they did not do so because of coal's technical superiority. On the contrary, the transition to coal took place in the face of a general preference for water.

Steam systems required coal in large quantities and at great expense, while a mill on a river could run year after year at very little cost.[20] Water was safer (steam mills tended to explode), simpler to operate, and less prone to breakdown. Until at least the 1830s, the regularity of a reliable waterwheel produced better cotton than did the unsteady power from a boiler.

To understand why steam became the norm, consider the proposal developed by the engineer Robert Thom in the 1830s for an ingenious system of waterways throughout Lancashire, capable of providing cheap, safe, and reliable power to all the mills in the area. '[B]e quit of these smoky and expensive engines!' he urged local capitalists, an injunction that expressed the consensus as to the relative value of water and steam.[21]

Yet Thom's venture, like similar projects, never came to fruition — not because his canals didn't work, but because, in order to capitalise on them, the mill owners needed to share a common resource, something that proved entirely beyond them. Despite the scheme's undoubted efficiencies, it failed because the local capitalists could not agree on who would pay the project's costs and on how the river's water would be apportioned. Private businesses simply could not work with a technology that rested on planning, co-ordination, and co-operation.[22]

Furthermore, the streams and rivers most suitable for powering mills generally ran through the countryside, which forced industrialists to establish their operations far from population centres. That presented them with immediate difficulties, since the inhabitants of rural districts often maintained a degree of aloofness from wage labour. If they hadn't been driven off the land, they probably still hadn't been inducted into the commodity economy entirely, perhaps producing their own food and clothing. As a result, they were less inclined to spend their waking hours spinning cotton in a textile factory.

How, then, might the proprietor of a rural mill source reliable staff to tend his water wheel? Some owners turned to 'apprentices' provided to them from the poorhouses: in essence, a system of forced labour, preying on destitute youths. But that didn't constitute a long-term solution, partly because reformers cracked down on a relationship pretty close to slavery, and partly because of the propensity of such 'apprentices' to escape or rebel.

Other owners created special 'colonies' near their mills, founding purpose-built communities to house a ready supply of labour. For a while, such company towns were touted as a solution to the upheavals besetting the cities. In the country, the argument went, labourers could be housed and schooled and educated according to the most modern principles so that they developed a paternal relationship with their employer that would see them toiling away loyally, even as the men in the cities walked out on strike.

Unfortunately, bitter experience established that, in the close quarters of a town centred on a single workplace, discontent tended, if anything, to spread more quickly. For all the advantages of water, industrialists did not feel inclined to maintain an expensive colony if their community became an incubator for rebellions against them.

As a result, as Sir Walter Scott noted disapprovingly, the once-thriving river mills suffered, as manufacturers shifted to the cities where they could abandon any pretence of paternalism and simply 'assemble five hundred workmen one week and dismiss them the next without having any ... further solicitude about their future fate than if they were so many old shuttles'.[23]

Coal-powered steam triumphed, in other words, because it didn't need to be installed adjacent to suitable waterways, but could be brought to the population centres and applied where workers were in abundance, something that mattered more than its widely acknowledged inferiority. Water might have been renewable, but it simply did not give the employers the social power they could obtain from the more flexible fossil fuels. A river could not drive the Iron Man because the machine was designed explicitly to 'strangle the Hydra of misrule', and so it needed the mobility of coal to perform its disciplinary mission.

The whole point of the steam-driven workplace was to ensure that men laboured as directed by devices that suddenly possessed unearthly volition. For professor Ure, this animation of the inhuman represented an enormous achievement. The modern factory, he said, unified labour, science, and capital, and thus 'form[ed] a body qualified to discharge its manifold functions by an intrinsic self-governing agency, like those of organic life'.[24]

It was like organic life, but it was decidedly not natural. The enchantment of the machine rather corresponded to the disenchantment of the human, transforming labour from a conscious engagement with the world into a mindless subservience to clanking pulleys and gears. In previous eras, work had meant men and women thinking as well as acting, forming a mental conception of their activity as they performed it. Now, though, thinking was controlled elsewhere, as the employers stripped as much skill and independence from factory jobs as possible.

As we have seen, humans interact with nature in a distinctive fashion. All creatures perform work to change their environment, but only humans consciously plan their work before they perform it. The purposeful component of our attitude to nature defines us as a species. Yet that was precisely what the new system challenged. 'The benignant power of steam,' Ure tells us, 'summons around him his myriads of willing menials, and assigns to each the regulated task ...'[25]

The owners no longer permitted employees to think about their work in a meaningful sense, confining them to a single activity, intended as a component of a plan that they were neither allowed nor expected to understand. The men and women of the factories were known as 'hands' because that was what they had become, mere appendages detached from minds. That separation fundamentally changed the human interaction with the world. By consolidating industrial management over labour, the mechanised factory accentuated the damage to ecological webs already disrupted by the expropriation of the population from the land.

In the pre-capitalist order, the control that ordinary men and women possessed over their labour made possible — indeed, in many cases, mandated — a sensitivity to the cycles of nature. The Indigenous people of Australia could enrich their existence only by learning about their environment and then using that knowledge to maintain their country. The extraordinary advances of the early nineteenth century served a very different purpose, as Ure made clear. The machines over which he rhapsodised transformed thinking people into drudges, working not according to any natural pattern, but rather toiling on whatever made most money for their employers.

The mill owners did not, of course, recognise that the coal they burned with such abandon would eventually threaten the well-being of the world. But they did know — for how could they not? — the environmental and social consequences of their fuel.

The conditions in the early-nineteenth-century steam mills were atrocious. Workers endured temperatures reaching 39 degrees, tending noisy, dangerous machines that not infrequently maimed or killed them. One publication in 1851 recorded how, within the previous three years, some 1,600 people had died as a result of boiler explosions.[26]

The effect on the natural world was just as marked.

When the French writer Alexis de Tocqueville visited the industrial town of Manchester in 1835, he described some 300,000 people working on steam-powered machinery, in a metropolis shrouded in smoke so thick that the sun could barely be seen.[27] It was, he declared, the most advanced city in the world — and, paradoxically, the most brutish, precisely because the new technologies were devoted not to giving people control over their lives, but rather to stripping them of all autonomy.

Around that time, the average life expectancy in the Manchester working class was said to be seventeen.[28] A decade or so later, the House of Commons responded to allegations about the toxicity of the smoke in the city. The MPs, many of whom themselves owned factories, rejected the complaints, in what is now a very familiar style, claiming that the ill effects had not been proven and, in any case, its 'suppression might materially injure important branches of our national industry'.[29]

Yet, though the parliamentarians scoffed at the notion that coal smoke might be dangerous, the city itself gave the lie to their assertions, with the wealthy housed in suburbs increasingly distant from industrial areas.[30] The money coming out of the factories enabled the privileged to build their villas far away from the hellish landscapes they created.

If the rich knew the damage being done by coal, so, too, did the poor.

In 1842, an unprecedented general strike led to half a million workers laying down their tools. The newspapers at the time referred to the dispute as 'the Plug Riots', because of a particular tactic adopted by the strikers. As they paraded through the factory districts, they called for the destruction of the steam engines they blamed for their poverty and oppression. To facilitate that destruction, activists pulled out the plugs by which steam was sealed in.

In some areas, they chanted as they marched, 'Stop the smoke!'[31]

Again, the strikers did not understand the greenhouse effect. But they did know that steam — and behind steam, coal — was weaponised against them; that it did not serve the interests of humanity in the way its advocates claimed; that, in fact, it had been integrated into the structures of industrial capital, and, as such, constituted a threat to the majority of ordinary people.

The novel *Frankenstein* can be read as a reflection of Shelley's liberal radicalism, with her monster a literary response to the rise of Luddism and similar movements.[32] On this reading, her book warns of the violence and death awaiting Britain's rulers, as the masses seek violent retribution for the treatment dished out to them.

Hence the monster's impassioned speech to its creator:

Are you to be happy, while I grovel in the intensity of my wretchedness? You can blast my other passions; but revenge remains—revenge, henceforth dearer than light or food! I may die; but first you, my tyrant and tormentor, shall curse the sun that gazes on your misery. Beware; for I am fearless, and therefore powerful.[33]

Yet there is another way to think of monstrosity in the age of stream, one that resonates with the preoccupations of the twenty-first century.

In 1842, for instance, the Chartist journal *Northern Star* explained how ordinary people in Britain had been barred from enjoying 'the choicest gifts of creation' by an industrial machine that, 'with its eternal thump, thump, thump, has been reducing, under the piston of the steam engine, the poor to powder'. The writer compared the technology deployed by the mill owners to a fairy-tale giant, grinding their bones to make his bread.[34]

Ure's Iron Man was constructed from metal and powered by coal. Yet, in another sense, it was built from the flesh of men, crudely hitched together — in the factory, it took charge of the workers' bodies and moved them this way and that, just as Ure's philosophical apparatus had made the dead weaver jerk.

The environmental destruction that ensued was not a consequence of science in the abstract, but rather the result of a specific technology that emerged entwined with industrial production. In different circumstances, scientific breakthroughs might have enabled men and women to care for the planet and each other, as they learned more about the world around them. In the context of the 1830s, it did the opposite, facilitating the release of carbon dioxide, in quantities that grew and grew and grew.

Again, the industrialists of the time did not understand just what they were releasing. Impelled by competition, they created, like Dr Frankenstein, a monster that took on a life of its own — and so now climate change confronts us as an external menace, precisely the kind of catastrophe you expect an Iron Man or similar supervillain to wreak on the planet.

Not every worker in the nineteenth century marched against smoke. Then, as now, some associated pollution with prosperity, and backed the expansion of the factories.[35] Nevertheless, it's important to remember that, in the early decades of the nineteenth century, there were ordinary men and women who warned about how the forces being set in motion would devastate humanity. That should be a source of hope. If, at the very onset of the fossil-fuel age, they could protest and resist, we can surely do the same today.

CHAPTER FIVE

Father Abraham versus Mrs Consumer

During fashion week in 2018, the American label Chromat staged a show in which glamorous young women tripped down the runway clutching pool noodles and packets of Flamin' Hot Cheetos. That year, Moschino's Jeremy Scott kitted out his models with moon boots and metallic PVC clothes reminiscent of B-grade sci-fi movies, while South Korean designer Kaimin equipped hers with pubic mohawk wigs.[1]

The bizarre, unwearable garments of high fashion seem, at first glance, further evidence of the superficiality of a wasteful and affluent society. According to the World Bank, the sector contributes nearly 20 per cent of industrial water pollution annually, consumes 25 per cent of chemicals produced worldwide, and releases 10 per cent of carbon emissions.[2] Designers stage their peculiar stunts, we might think, because modern consumers require constant titillation — and, to please their jaded sensibilities, the billion-dollar clothing industry chokes the planet with unnecessary garbage.

Yet the history of fashion reveals something entirely different about consumer society and its emergence.

In 1991, two German hikers trekking the Öztal Alps on the

Austrian–Italian border found the body of a forty-five-year-old man. He was not a lost climber, but the victim of a murder, killed by an arrow fired into his back in approximately 3300 BC. The mummified corpse (popularly dubbed 'Ötzi') revealed an amazing trove of information about the ancient past, including about its fashion. Ötzi possessed a surprisingly modern outfit: a coat (fashioned from goat and sheep hide) that reached down to his knees, and two separate sets of leggings of the same material. As undergarments, he wore a hide loincloth fastened with a calfskin belt equipped with a pouch. He protected his head with a bearskin cap; his shoes were constructed from string netting stuffed with grass and layered with deer hide. The clothing, without which he could never have survived in an alpine climate, showed signs of constant use: the leggings and coat had, for instance, been mended, probably by Ötzi himself.

The care he had lavished on the garments that had kept him alive demonstrated a particular attitude to clothing. In pre-capitalist societies, people husbanded resources carefully. They made the items that they used; they knew how much time and effort went into each of them.

That's why the term 'consume', in its early-English usage, invariably possessed a pejorative sense: it meant, as Raymond Williams points out, 'to destroy, to use up, to waste, to exhaust' (as in the phrase 'consumed by fire').[3] Correspondingly, in Old English, 'thrift' emerged to mean a 'thriving condition' or a 'means to prosperity', a word associated with proper household management.

Early capitalism began with the circulation of relatively few commodities. Most people still made a substantial proportion of their own necessities. They grew vegetables, raised chickens for eggs and meat, and kept cows for milk. Householders might have purchased cloth, thread, or other items from stores. Yet they brewed their own lager and baked their own bread — and they sewed and repaired clothing. A visit to a tailor constituted an unusual extravagance for anyone but the rich.

Even into the nineteenth century, most Americans wore pants, dresses, or shirts that had been sewn by themselves or by someone they knew. A government report in the 1810s, for instance, estimated that some two-thirds of the garments worn in America were still created inside the private home.

Benjamin Franklin's 1758 pamphlet *The Way to Wealth* demonstrated the attitudes associated with such a lifestyle. Franklin's text appeared in 145 editions in seven languages before the end of the eighteenth century. Its extraordinary influence makes it a useful source for the development of ideas about appropriate consumption in the early-capitalist era.[4]

In a letter to a friend, Franklin explained why he wrote the tract. He wanted, he said, to encourage 'Industry and Frugality among the Lower People'.[5] Most of *The Way to Wealth* consists of lectures about the necessity for hard work — and plenty of it. Franklin's wise Father Abraham, around whose maxims Franklin constructs his text, tells his readers that 'sloth makes all things difficult but industry all easy', an adage repeated throughout the book in various tedious ways.

Yet, strikingly, Father Abraham also fulminates against consumption.

'You may think, perhaps,' he warns sternly, 'that a little tea, or a little punch now and then, diet a little more costly, clothes a little finer, and a little entertainment now and then, can be no great matter; but remember, many a little makes a mickle'.[6]

Though Weber famously hails Franklin as embodying the spirit of capitalism, his ethos ('Beware of little expenses!') doesn't at all reflect modern attitudes. One can't, for instance, imagine Father Abraham, with his disdain for 'clothes a little finer', approving of Chromat's merkins. Franklin wrote in an era in which generalised commodity production remained relatively new, and when working people were still adjusting to a very different kind of life. *The Way to Wealth* was circulated, in particular, among communities in which commodity relationships remained novel, intended to acclimatise them to new thinking. In England, for instance, Lord Shaftesbury's Labourers' Friend Society republished *The Way to Wealth* under the title 'Advice to Labourers', with an introduction suggesting that Franklin's maxims should be framed and displayed in every worker's cottage.[7]

The development of the economic order changed the meaning of frugality. Feudal tailors could make clothes for the same clients all their lives, but capitalist textile factories needed their enterprises to expand. Competition between individual manufacturers drove each to further accumulation. Expansion required new markets, new methods, and an ever-widening sphere of circulation. That meant modes of consumption.

American clothing provides a good illustration of the ways in which such markets were created. Crucially, the industry we know today did not develop simply in response to the demands of the masses. Contrary to what we're often told, the shifts in production were not to serve the wants of ordinary people. Rather, expanding businesses required new markets and often found them via coercion, with the initial customers for the 'ready-made' garments we now take for granted coming from those physically prevented from making their own clothes.

In the early 1800s, establishments known as 'slop shops' sprung up in port cities such as Boston, New York, Philadelphia, and Baltimore, catering to sailors seeking outfits when they reached shore. Seafarers would be expected to repair their clothes at sea; but, by the end of a long voyage, their much-patched dungarees might not be appropriate on land, or sustainable for another journey. Hence the need for crude 'slop clothes', serving, as historians Stuart and Elizabeth Ewen say, a workforce prevented, by the nature of its labour, from producing clothes for itself.[8]

The discovery of gold in the American west opened a second market for ready-made clothes, with miners — single men lacking the wherewithal to clothe themselves — looking for durable work attire. Today's jeans, for instance, evolved from the tough denim pants sold to men labouring in the goldfields.

The development of clothing as an industry depended, in particular, on slavery, in a complicated two-way relationship. The plantation system grew to sell cotton to the English textile factories of the Industrial Revolution, with their increased productivity creating a fierce hunger for raw materials. The new factory machines — and the social relations associated with them — soon found their way to America, in part because the Boston businessman Francis Cabot Lowell stole Arkwright's invention in the course of an 1810 industrial-espionage mission to Manchester.

The American textile factories required markets of their own. On the early plantations, owners forced some of the slaves to stitch for others, making as many clothes for the enslaved as garments for free men. From about the 1840s, industrialists recognised a market in crude pants and shirts for slaves: the I M Singer Company developed what it called a 'new, improved sewing machine especially adapted to the making up of Negro clothing'; the Louisiana Steam Clothing Manufactory boasted of making 'plantation clothing, on a very large scale'; and in New Orleans, the Folgar and Black Company advertised to planters that they would 'find it greatly to their advantage to purchase their clothing ready-made' for slaves. The owners could, indeed, increase their yield of profitable cotton if those slaves previously devoted to mending could be forced back out on the fields. Slavery, then, spurred on the US garment industry, as businesses in New York competed to supply ready-made outfits to what was literally a captive market.[9]

The Civil War that brought slavery to an end then created an entirely different opportunity. Both the Union and Confederate forces needed cheap, durable clothes in which their soldiers could fight. The conflict proved a massive boon for manufacturers, with the early factories ideally suited to churning out huge quantities of identical trousers and shirts. The war normalised ready-made garments in the eyes of the public, allowed textile manufacturers to develop expertise in producing clothes, and established the notion of standardised sizing.

When peace came, the firms that had profited during the conflict reinvented themselves, offering clothes to labourers flocking to the big cities. In their rural homes, such people wore clothes made within the family. But as they found jobs in factories, their circumstances changed. Where their old lives in the country revolved around household production, making a new outfit in a cheap lodging house or an urban slum became a far more challenging proposition.

Though fashion had once been the domain of the wealthy, by about the 1880s, working-class people could purchase clothes that at least nodded to current trends and designs. The suit was developed as a fashionable, ready-made garment for men, while women could buy cheap imitations of the cloaks, bustles, and crinolines worn by the upper class. Wholesalers such as Julius Rosenwald — later the head of Sears, Roebuck and Co. — established business models in which the marketing of pants and shirts mattered as much as manufacturing them: a forerunner of today's industry.

In the American context, early fashion possessed a certain democratic veneer, its advertising suggesting that, when they purchased chic garments, working people could live like the elite. To understand this, the history of clothing must be analysed alongside the history of work — for, if mass consumption was enabled by mass production, it was also required by it.

As capitalism expanded, the tendencies nascent in the early

nineteenth century developed to a monstrous degree. The factories that Ure lauded grew, becoming larger and more intricate, while the ideas he avowed evolved into more complex systems of control. These were codified in the work of Frederick Winslow Taylor, a former engineer turned efficiency consultant.

In *The Principles of Scientific Management* (1911), Taylor illustrates the methods of the twentieth century by discussing how, at the Bethlehem Steel Company, he made a group of pig-iron handlers — men responsible for picking up and carrying heavy lumps of metal — increase their production. Initially, he says, he studied them all, making inquiries into their characters, habits, and ambitions. Then he selected a particular target: a worker whom he describes as a 'little Pennsylvania Dutchman' called Schmidt (we never learn his first name), a man he assessed as both physically strong and keen for extra money.

Taylor asks Schmidt if he is a 'high-priced man' — that is, someone who gets more wages for doing the same work.

Unsurprisingly, Schmidt answers in the affirmative.

Taylor points at a supervisor.

'Well, if you are a high-priced man, you will do exactly as this man tells you tomorrow, from morning till night.'[10]

He explains that, when the supervisor instructs Schmidt to lift a 'pig' (or lump of steel) and carry it, Schmidt is to do so. When the supervisor says to rest, he is to rest. All through the day, he is to unquestioningly obey, with no complaints, questions, or back talk.

Taylor agrees that a similar dialogue would be 'rather rough' if applied to someone educated or even intelligent. But, he insists, 'with a man of the mentally sluggish type of Schmidt', it was 'appropriate and not unkind', since it focussed his attention on the promised high wages and not on an intensity of work that, in other circumstances, he would consider impossible.[11]

The Principles of Scientific Management does not record Schmidt's feelings. We learn only that, henceforth, he works precisely as instructed ('Now pick up a pig and walk!'), and, as a result, moves far more pig iron than the other men, most of whom are duly sacked.

For Taylor, the episode illustrates a number of conclusions. Pig-iron handling is, he says, such a crude job that 'an intelligent gorilla' could perform it. Schmidt, though, cannot: according to Taylor, the kind of man suited to carrying iron 'is too stupid to properly train himself'.[12]

Schmidt's supposed incapacity turns out to be a trait shared with his colleagues and indeed his entire class. Working men, Taylor says, learn their jobs in an ad hoc fashion, whereas efficient production requires a manager to 'develop a science for each element of a man's work', replacing the 'old rule-of-thumb method' with a time-and-motion analysis. Only bosses can develop, say, the 'science of pig-iron handling',[13] because, Taylor explains, workers deliberately prevent efficient labour, fearing (quite correctly) that their jobs will be sped up if they do them faster.

Employers must, then, take all control from workers, plan the labour process down to the most granular detail, and then force the men to perform precisely as mandated. That is what scientific management entails.

Taylorism thus expresses the logic of commodified labour power at an even more developed stage. Where Ure removes the autonomy of craftsmen, Taylor removes the autonomy of all workers, skilled and unskilled alike. Management, he claims, possesses the right and the responsibility to control both the conception and execution of the work process, whether for a ditch digger or a phone canvasser.

In his book, Taylor compares himself to a conservationist. He mourns the felling of the forests, the erosion of the soil, and the disappearance of coal and iron deposits. In such a time of destruction, he says, the least he can do is prevent the waste of 'human effort' in factories.[14]

Yet Taylor's 'conservation' does not mean the development of any relationship in which earth and trees might be nurtured rather than degraded and abused. Rather than reintegrating into nature's cycles the labour by which men and women engage with the world, he seeks the opposite: an intensification of the separation between people and the results of their work, so that they toil harder and faster, following without question instructions by managers devoted to capital's expansion.

Taylor mentions, in passing, that the iron lumped by Schmidt was in particular demand because of the outbreak of the Spanish–American War, which created a demand for armaments. But the Bethlehem Steel Company did not care whether its metal became deadly weapons or hospital beds or art sculptures, just as it did not mind whether its output devastated or preserved the environment. It wanted a return on its capital, an outcome measurable quantitatively and not qualitatively. Taylor's own writings document how much employees loathed his methods, and how bitterly they fought their imposition, which only became possible after a gruelling, vicious campaign to break their resistance. Their hatred stemmed not only from their (entirely correct) fear that Taylorist practices would mandate general speed-ups and, eventually, redundancies. It also expressed their hostility to practices that stripped their work of purpose. When Taylor described lumping as an activity suited to a gorilla, he unwittingly articulated the dehumanising consequences of what he demanded, a system that eroded the distinction between the instinctive acts of animals and the planned activities of humans.

When they finally acquiesced to the new rules, workers gave up any lingering sense of labour as a meaningful activity, and accepted that, in the factory, the hand and the brain were to be entirely separate, divorced in a way that was profoundly anti-human. The men now worked like animals, rather than people, driven by an external compulsion rather than their own design.[15]

Schmidt could not, as Taylor emphasised again and again, even choose something as basic as when he rested after lifting the iron. Submitting to management's total control, he and his workmates resigned themselves to tedium. Their work — that fundamentally human practice — became dead to them.

Its death made other activities take on a new life.

In pre-class society, no divide separated 'work' and 'leisure', both of which were integrated into the daily routine. People sang as they gathered fruit; they danced for pleasure as well as to ensure a successful harvest; they worshiped the animals they hunted. The banality of Taylorised labour created an insurmountable barrier between working and non-working time, such that the latter became infinitely more precious.

Schmidt might have been, as Taylor describes him, 'so stupid and so phlegmatic that he more nearly resembles in his mental make-up the ox than any other type'. Yet we learn, in passing, that this supposedly moronic fellow had bought himself a 'small plot of ground' and is 'putting up the walls of a little house for himself'.[16]

It was, we presume, this activity — something he did on his own, for his own sake — that compensated him for being treated like a bird or an insect. In that respect, he was fortunate. Taylorism would, in due course, make such creative pursuits — the activities by which a previous generation supplemented wage labour — less and less tenable.

In the nineteenth century, weavers' skills enabled them to make their own clothes. In the twentieth century, garment workers performed one simple activity all day long, a task with no direct application to the needs of their own household. While 'work' and 'leisure' became opposites, they also mirrored each other, with the latter defined by measured time just as much as the former. Workers, just like bosses, relied on commodities: for their food, their clothing, and to render their leisure time meaningful. They bought ready-made meals so as not to waste precious hours of freedom cooking. They paid for beers at the pub to relax; they took their partners to shows on a Friday night.

Taylor tells us his 'workmen will not submit to … more rigid standardization and will not work extra hard, unless they receive extra pay for doing it'.[17] That was, in a sense, the Taylorist bargain: higher wages enabled workers to afford the activities through which they coped with the odious hours of wage labour.

The idea — meaningless work facilitating increased consumption — manifested itself most classically in the factories designed by the car magnate Henry Ford.

The early automobile industry had relied on artisanal tinkerers, backyard inventors experimenting with the possibilities of the new technology. In 1903, when Ford established his first factory, cars were still assembled piece by piece by craftsmen, usually by men who had taught themselves in bicycle and carriage shops.

Ford distinguished himself by breaking down, in Taylorist fashion, the construction of his iconic Model T into a series of simple tasks. His mass automotive production mirrored the conveyer-belt system used in the abattoirs of Chicago, where an assembly line meant carcasses moved to butchers rather than the butchers moving to carcasses, as had previously been the case. This innovation meant that, within three months, the time taken to assemble a Model T was reduced to one-tenth of previous records. Eventually, the company could, in a single day, roll out as many cars as had once been manufactured in a year.[18] The resulting low prices enabled working Americans to buy automobiles, and so helped normalise car culture across the nation.

Yet Ford's employees loathed the new regime, and, from about 1910, began to leave him. When he instituted his first assembly line, the trickle of resignations became a flood, with so many workers quitting that Ford's business struggled to operate, let alone expand.[19]

The reason was simple. Those early mechanics loved cars. They operated as artisans, in control of every aspect of the vehicles on which they laboured. In the earliest automobile companies, they could still work creatively, solving problems and developing skills. They liked the fact that their tasks had purpose; they wanted to exercise their minds as well as their hands, in activities that made sense to them. In 1910, other firms still permitted something more like craftsmanship, and so, when Ford implemented his assembly line, the men went to them.

In response, Ford created the industrial model that came to be known as Fordism. With tremendous publicity, he announced that, henceforth, his company would pay its workers five dollars a day — a sizeable increase, and substantially in excess of anything available from rival manufacturers.

In essence, Ford dangled the same deal in front of his men that Taylor had made to poor Schmidt. By inflating salaries, he fended off a unionisation drive and obtained a huge pool of available labour, as the men accepted tedium and regimentation in exchange for more money. He also achieved a real intensification of production. Like the pig-iron lumpers, the Ford employees were keen to remain high-priced men, even as the line sped up and up and up.

Competition meant that the Fordist model spread throughout the auto industry, and then throughout manufacturing as a whole. Production speeds accelerated accordingly, with factories churning out commodities at rates previously believed impossible.

The process worker, performing the same empty task over and over again, became the paradigm for wage labour in the early twentieth century.

But the strategy implemented by Ford rested on more than just Taylorised conditions. Fordism also meant a recognition of workers as markets for the products they built. The man on the assembly line produced commodities, but he and his family also consumed them, simply because, increasingly, they had no choice. The abattoirs lured thousands of immigrants from Eastern Europe to jobs in Chicago. In their villages in their own countries, they might have raised and slaughtered pigs or chickens in the backyard. But they could not tend livestock in urban Chicago — and so instead they bought canned meat sourced from the slaughterhouses in which they toiled. The women who sewed all day in the garment factories paid for dresses with their wages; the Ford workers drove Ford automobiles.

They could afford the new commodities; they also needed them, since the old ways of household production were no longer practical. A factory hand drawn to Detroit by the automobile industry did not have the energy to milk a cow in the morning, even if he had room to graze the animal or the skills to tend it. He and his family purchased their milk, just like they purchased everything else, with the market now the source of their psychological, social, and material needs.

The dependence of ordinary people on the new commodities from assembly lines became an important ideological prop for the companies themselves. In 1937, the Chevrolet Motor Company released a propaganda film entitled *From Dawn to Sunset*, portraying its employees as happy consumers as well as happy workers. The movie showed Chevrolet employees collecting their pay, and then, with excited wives and children in tow, heading to stores to buy, not only cars, but furniture, bicycles, and fashionable clothes.

'America has a ready purse and gives eager acceptance to what the men of motors have built,' explains the narrator, before concluding that the nation was set to enjoy 'a prosperity greater than history has ever known'.[20]

In reality, the new consumption did not rest on such a simple and mutually beneficial partnership between labour and capital. After all, one reason the companies pushed for such increases in productivity was that by making the staples of working-class life cheaper, they tended to decrease the value of labour power and thus wages.

Not surprisingly, during this period, the auto industry was, in fact, wracked by industrial disputes (including the iconic Flint sit-down strike of 1936), in part because work in the factories remained so deadening. That tedium was, indeed, built into the Fordist system, with the purchase of commodities becoming so meaningful precisely because working life felt so empty.

If, all day long, the phlegmatic Schmidt moves lumps of iron according to the minute instructions compiled by Taylor's assistant, we should not be surprised that he longs to dress sharply on Friday night, turning his wages into the clothes that advertisers have associated with freedom, success, and power. The desires into which marketers tapped bubbled up from the monotony and impotence of a labour entirely controlled by others, in ways that changed attitudes towards consumption.

Consider the book published by the home economist Christine Frederick in 1929 under the title *Selling Mrs Consumer*.

Frederick offers an updated version of Benjamin Franklin's tract, an attempt to provide prescriptive economic ethics for ordinary citizens in a very different era. In an earlier phase of capitalism, the home was a productive unit, in which both men and women worked. Now, Frederick says, the husband earns the money through wage labour, while the woman runs the household. Her management consists entirely of buying commodities: she is the 'Mrs Consumer' of the title.

As a result, the new American woman behaved very differently from her old-fashioned sisters in Europe, so much so that French women visiting the United States generally expressed their shock at the waste they witnessed all around them. That was because Americans bought 'so many, many things that are simple to make in the home and that no foreign woman thinks of buying, and buy them far more often, because we discard them before their use is anywhere near exhausted'.[21]

Frederick does not, however, regard this wastefulness and extravagance as problematic. On the contrary, she blames the abstemious and snooty French. The dawning of the 'machine and power era' makes frugality a vice, she says, an unjustified break on progress. Any lingering guilt about discarding unfinished products should be rejected as entirely misplaced, with waste now a positive virtue.

It's an astonishing shift from the ethos extolled by Franklin, a complete reversal of attitudes. Where Father Abraham scolds eighteenth-century Americans for craving 'silks and satins, scarlet and velvets',[22] rather than necessities, Frederick urges their twentieth-century descendants to buy and keep buying, insisting they should not only consume but deliberately squander, with their wastefulness central to the American economy.

'[I]t is absurd,' she says, 'to expect us to produce more and not at the same time expect us to spend more ... Mrs. Consumer and her attitude toward change is the key to the situation; the dial which registers how fast we can move. If only she would creatively waste more rather than less!'[23]

Frederick's book might have been something of an outlier, with its overt enthusiasm for profligacy an almost deliberate provocation. But it foreshadowed what would come in the post-war era — a massive and unprecedented campaign to foster consumption.

That history tells a quite different story from the one we usually hear. Ordinary people did not indulge in excess out of greed and selfishness, but because they were given no other choice. Consumers were made, not born — created, deliberately, by a system that needed commodities constantly exchanged. And that should give us hope. What can be made can always be unmade. A different kind of society might require neither the parsimony of

Father Abraham nor the profligacy of Mrs Consumer, but instead encourage the conscious allocation of resources where they were needed — precisely the attitude shown by most ordinary people prior to capitalism.

CHAPTER SIX

Our Life Will Be Disposable

In his classic novel *Brave New World*, Aldous Huxley describes a dystopia in which recorded voices subliminally prepare infants for their future role as consumers.

'I do love flying, I do love having new clothes,' the voices whisper. 'But old clothes are beastly. We always throw away old clothes. Ending is better than mending. Ending is better than mending.'[1]

Huxley's messages eerily presage genuine slogans used by advertisers in America after the Second World War. In his book *The Waste Makers*, Vance Packard lists some of them:

'Buy days mean paydays … and paydays mean better days!'
'You auto buy now.'
'Buy now—the job you save may be your own.'
'Buy and be happy.'
'Buy, buy, buy; it's your patriotic duty.'
'Buy your way to prosperity.'[2]

Today, such imprecations sound especially grotesque, because we know they coincided with what environmentalists call the 'Great Acceleration': the era in which all the measures of humanity's impact on nature, from carbon emissions to ocean acidification to deforestation, climbed and climbed and climbed. In the years after the Second World War, every statistic shows a phenomenal growth in the rate at which human beings degraded the environment.[3]

Yet, as the dystopian advertisements recorded by Packard suggests, the new resource-heavy mode of consumer capitalism did not develop on its own. Conspicuous consumption was not a response by obliging manufacturers to the instinctive desire of ordinary people for more. The business leaders of the period were under no illusions. They did not see Americans as innately greedy. On the contrary, they worried that, even after Fordism, Americans were not sufficiently rapacious — and so they launched a deliberate and prolonged campaign to change them.

The result was what scientists from the International Geosphere-Biosphere Program called 'the most rapid transformation of the human relationship with the natural world in the history of humankind'.[4]

The Second World War re-ignited the American economy after the Depression, with a huge Keynesian-style injection of revenue, mostly connected to the war effort. 'Powerful enemies must be out-fought and out-produced,' Franklin Roosevelt had told the nation a few weeks after Japan's attack on Pearl Harbor. 'It is not enough to turn out just a few more planes, a few more tanks, a few more guns, a few more ships than can be turned out by our enemies.'[5]

The assembly lines duly manufactured the materials of war at a staggering rate. America built 60,000 aircraft in 1942 and 125,000 in 1943, a period in which it constructed 120,000 tanks and 55,000 anti-aircraft guns. The automotive industry, in particular, devoted itself to military production, and, in the process, reconstructed itself. In the 1940s, Ford's average car comprised some 15,000 parts. The B-24 Liberator bomber had 1,550,000 parts — and, during the war, one B-24 came off the production line every sixty-three minutes.[6]

Not surprisingly, at the end of the Second World War, many politicians feared the US might slip back into Depression. Without the need for bombers or tanks, or, for that matter, military cars, what would happen to the new assembly lines? The location of fresh markets became a national priority. The result was the expansion and consolidation of the new American empire, in a context in which the decline of the old European powers had been definitively established.

In 1950, the National Security Council drafted a secret document called NSC-68, which urged higher armaments spending, in part as a way to forestall an economic downturn. This so-called military Keynesianism relied on a renewed expansion of the American defence forces to soak up resources and thus stimulate demand. After the outbreak of the Korean War, defence spending remained at an astonishing 12 per cent of GDP throughout the 1950s, and then 10 per cent during the 1960s.

But American statesmen also reappraised the market potential within the US itself. Mrs Consumer might be buying, but she wasn't, they decided, buying enough. Americans, the corporate leaders concluded, needed to use up resources more quickly, so as to create the demand that kept the assembly lines rolling. Bedevilled by over-production, they decided that, as Packard quipped, 'the way to end glut was to produce gluttons'.[7]

In the mid-1950s, the marketing consultant Victor Lebow explained the new situation, stressing the importance of what he called 'forced consumption'. In the *Journal of Retailing*, he explained that the productivity of the economy required consumption to become a way of life: 'We need things consumed, burned up, worn out, replaced, and discarded at an ever-increasing rate.'[8]

The president of the appliance manufacturers Servel Inc declared that Americans should have two refrigerators in every home; the American Home Laundry Manufacturers Association explained the necessity of two washers and two dryers; the Plumbing Fixture Manufacturers Association argued that every room in the house needed its own toilet; and, inevitably, the Douglas Fir Plywood Association insisted that every family should have two homes in which to fit all their new stuff.[9]

Consuming more was not enough. Americans were also required to consume more often. Corporations systematically embraced the notion of psychological obsolescence, inducing buyers to feel dissatisfied with items they already owned, even if those items remained entirely functional.

Louis Cheskin of the Color Research Institute explained the program: 'Most design changes are made not for improving the product, either aesthetically or functionally, but for making it obsolete.'[10]

By the late 1950s, Ford was employing a former clothing stylist to plan new looks for cars that remained essentially the same each year.[11] In 1959, a discussion of psychological obsolescence in *Dun's Review and Modern Industry* revealed the cynicism of the method. 'The trick isn't foolproof,' the author explained, 'but it ought to work a good part of the time — and perhaps can even be planned, assuring the manufacturer of a large, steadily increasing replacement market.'[12]

But the journal also cautioned that success required 'a decrease in the durability of the product'. In other words, manufacturers needed to complement psychological obsolescence by designing for so-called planned obsolescence: in essence, making products that did not last.[13]

Engineers constructing radios, for instance, began to calculate 'death dates' — that is, the time by which their units would fail and compel the owner to buy replacements. One writer in *Design News* exulted this 'planned existence spans of products' as 'the greatest economic boost to the American economy since the origination of time payments',[14] while the general manager at Frigidaire hailed it as the most important single factor for 'the growth and vitality of the appliance industry, the automobile industry, and many others'.[15]

In 1958, the industrial designer Brooks Stevens discussed the situation with extraordinary bluntness:

> Our whole economy is based on planned obsolescence, and everybody who can read without moving his lips should know it by now. We make good products, we induce people to buy them, and next year we deliberately introduce something that will make those products old fashioned, out of date, obsolete. We do that for the soundest reason: to make money.[16]

The reason might have been 'sound' economically, but it dramatically increased humanity's environmental footprint — as, indeed, it was designed to do. The pioneer ecologist Barry Commoner noted that almost all of America's worst pollution problems became either apparent or far worse in the post-war years, a direct consequence of the new resource-heavy economy.[17]

The same tendency could be identified around the world, as the systems of intensified consumption spread. When, in the early 2000s, scientists looked at atmospheric carbon dioxide, ozone depletion, species extinctions, loss of forests, and similar measures over the last 250 years, they discovered that every trend showed a gradual rise from the mid-eighteenth century and then a sharp spike from about 1950.

Of course, the Great Acceleration did not come from nowhere. Many of the techniques that underpinned post-war consumerism were already well known in certain sectors of the economy, a logical development of management thinking. As far back as 1927, General Motors introduced a yearly style-change in its cars, while Marmon, Jordan, and Hudson, and (eventually) GM began marketing to the 'two-car family'. In the same period, the radio makers Atwater Kent suggested that children would sleep better with their own set playing soothing music while the parents listened to jazz in a different room; Gruen told men they needed two watches; and soap manufacturers had made the case for multiple baths in a single day.[18]

Yet such campaigns had not always been successful, partly because they conflicted with ordinary people's deeply held beliefs about appropriate consumption. Despite Fordism, most purchasers did not like waste, while most workers preferred to labour on commodities that lasted. Furthermore, during the Second World War, the government had recognised the importance of conservation, with the Office of Price Administration publicising slogans such as 'If you don't need it, don't buy it!' and 'Use it Up, Wear it Out, Make it Do or Do Without!'[19]

But the declaration of peace had given way, almost at once, to a new conflict — the struggle against communism. And, in that war, consumption played a quite different role.

After the Second World War, a strike wave gripped America, even as tensions with the Soviet Union increased. Charles E Wilson, the head of General Electric, suggested that the problems of the United States at this time could be summed up as 'Russia abroad, labour at home.' Economic expansion was understood as the key to resolving both.

Yet, throughout the 1950s, American leaders despaired at their inability to match the success of the Soviet economy. In *Foreign Affairs* in 1953, Peter Wiles said bluntly that communism was beating capitalism in terms of its rate of growth — the factor judged most significant at the time.[20]

The focus on individual consumption reframed the debate, to the advantage of the Americans.

In 1959, vice-president Richard Nixon and the Russian leader, Nikita Khrushchev, walked together through the kitchen of a supposedly 'typical American house' at an exhibition at Sokolniki Park in Moscow.

'I want to show you this kitchen,' said Nixon. 'It's like those of houses in California. See that built-in washing machine?'

'We have such things,' growled Khrushchev, somewhat unconvincingly.[21]

When the vice-president showed off the modern American display kitchen, he boasted that the appliances made 'life easier for women' and that the house was affordable even for steel workers (who were currently on strike).

'Your American houses,' Khrushchev shot back, 'are built to last only twenty years so builders can sell new houses at the end. We build firmly. We build for our children and grandchildren.'

But Nixon was not all discomforted by Khrushchev's reference to planned obsolescence. He explained that, after twenty years, Americans wanted a new house and a kitchen. 'The American system,' he said, 'is designed to take advantage of new inventions and new techniques.'[22]

For Nixon, the marketing methods that fostered intensified consumption were not evidence of chicanery or extravagance. On the contrary, they proved American superiority. The Soviet economy might be growing more quickly (and even, perhaps, building more firmly), but the American economy was delivering for workers when socialism wasn't — because, and not in spite of, its wastefulness.

'The best trained and most talented members of our advanced society,' explained Robert Lekachman in 1960, 'earn their excellent livings by persuading fellow citizens that they are really discontented with the serviceable commodities they already possess.'[23]

But that wasn't necessarily a problem, as the resource-heavy suburban lifestyle became emblematic of the 'American way', and consumption took on a particular moral and political meaning. A few decades earlier, Christine Frederick had urged Mrs Consumer to embrace waste for the good of the economy. In the Cold War, the same habits became emblematic not simply of prosperity, but also of individualism, freedom, and patriotism. Mass production meant, the argument went, that Americans could deliver what the Soviets only promised, meeting the needs of workers almost before they were articulated.[24]

The public embrace of consumption was, in other words, facilitated by an intense ideological campaign in the context of the Cold War; but even then, it did not necessarily proceed as smoothly as manufacturers would have liked.

In the 1950s, planned obsolescence reached its natural conclusion with the development of the fully disposable commodity, as assembly lines rolled out an array of products (such as diapers, razors, and cooking utensils) designed to be used once and tossed away. Single-use items proliferated so quickly that the company Standard Packaging could adopt the slogan, 'Tomorrow, more than ever, our life will be "disposable".'[25]

Disposability also became standard with packaging. In the past, shoppers had often purchased from bulk bins or barrels, while manufacturers saw the reusability of their tins, jars, and other containers as a selling point. But in the post-war era, that changed. Mass production and the development of synthetic materials created new opportunities for embedding marketing on wrappers and coverings, even as disposability encouraged consumers to bin the item and buy another one. As the head of Standard Packaging explained, 'Everything we make is thrown away.'[26]

Disposability rested, in particular, on the rise of plastic, the production of which tripled in the US between 1940 and 1945. Cheap, infinitely pliable, and colourful, the new material was a boon to manufacturers. 'Plastic is wholly swallowed up in the fact of being used,' wrote an astonished Roland Barthes in the early

1950s. '[U]ltimately, objects will be invented for the sole pleasure of using them.'[27]

And so it proved.

The most recent figures put the quantity of plastic entering the ocean at some eight million metric tons every year, while microplastics have been discovered atop the highest mountains, under the deepest oceans, and within the human gut.

From the very start, manufacturers recognised that, given the speed at which plastic could be created, the creation of a surplus posed an obvious problem, especially since synthetic resins could take up to a thousand years to break down. Corporations adopted the usual solution: at the 1956 conference of the Society of the Plastics Industry (SPI), a speaker urged 'low cost, big volume, practicability, and expendability' on his fellows.

'Your future,' he told them, 'is in the garbage wagon.'[28]

To rally ordinary people behind this unlikely slogan, plastics producers immediately after the war ran a major educational campaign to sell consumers on the virtues of their new substance. Looking back from the vantage point of 1956, the editor of the trade journal *Modern Plastics* acknowledged that 'not a single solid market for plastics in existence today was eagerly waiting for these materials'. On the contrary, each new plastic product faced 'either fearsome competition from vested materials or inertia and misunderstanding in acceptance, all of which had to be overcome before plastics gained a market'.[29]

The problem wasn't simply to persuade the public to acquire plastic. It was also to persuade them to get rid of it.

Take the plastic bag. By 1958, makers of polyethylene film had sold a billion of the new bags, which were particularly embraced by the dry-cleaning industry. But that year and the next, a rash of newspaper reports documented the role of polyethylene in the suffocation of as many as eighty children (as well as multiple suicides of adults). The public hostility was immense, and was reflected in the tenor of the media coverage. One reporter described plastic bags as 'murderous'; the *New York Journal* complained that 'an almost invisible peril hangs loosely over the helpless heads of the nation's infants'; and the *San Francisco News* urged the nation to 'Ban the Bags'.[30]

Even as the Society of the Plastics Industry protested that there was no 'mysterious built-in danger' to bags and that they did not 'literally reach out to ensnare children', calls for legislative action proliferated. Plastic bags were only saved by a major publicity campaign by the SPI and extensive lobbying of state and local lawmakers explicitly to prevent restrictive regulations.[31]

'Our job was and should always be open plastics markets and keep them open,' the SPI's lawyer said.[32]

Crucially, infants were able to choke on the bags because people intuitively recycled them, just as they'd done with cloth or other containers in the past. In fact, the practice of re-use was, initially, taken for granted, even by the industry.

In 1956, for instance, *The New York Times* told readers how clear plastic bags should be cleaned inside and out with a few dabs of a sudsy sponge. 'Dry the bag promptly,' it explained, 'and it will stay lovely for many seasons to come.'[33]

A spokesperson for Du Pont might have protested that these lovely bags were actually 'made and costed to be disposable', but it took some time before ordinary people could be induced to discard them as quickly as the manufacturers wanted.

This was a general phenomenon. In the late 1950s, the industry journal *Modern Plastic* was still bemoaning its customers' tendency to re-use plastic drinking cups. Yet it consoled its readers that 'it is only a matter of time until the public accepts the plastics cups as more convenient containers that are completely discardable'.[34] That promise proved utterly correct. Today, best estimates suggest that some 500 billion plastic cups get used annually — and almost none of them are recycled.[35]

Similarly, plastic could only replace the previously ubiquitous paper bags in American supermarkets in 1976 after the industry stared down the initial widespread hostility of shoppers. To facilitate the introduction of plastic, the 'bag companies reached out directly to stores with educational programs to help grocers overcome shoppers' distaste for the bags'.[36]

The common narrative about a lazy public choosing plastic with no consideration for anything else bears little relationship to historical fact. How, then, did it become so widely accepted?

CHAPTER SEVEN

It Looks Like a Green Winter

On 31 March 1929, a group of fashionable young women marched down Fifth Avenue. They were, very ostentatiously, smoking cigarettes.[1]

To understand why that mattered, we need to recognise the culture war taking place over tobacco at the time. Prior to the First World War, American men puffed cigars or pipes, took snuff, or chewed plugs. Pre-rolled cigarettes were less common — and often considered effeminate, foreign, or eccentric.

The war changed that. In the trenches, nicotine killed boredom during the long periods of tedium, and offered comfort after moments of terror. In recognition of the drug's utility, General Pershing, the leader of the American troops, pleaded with his superiors to send 'tobacco, more tobacco — even more than food'.[2] He got his wish. Tobacco rolling machines had been patented as far back as 1881, and the new factories answered wartime demand with a seemingly limitless supply of pre-rolled cigarettes, providing a more convenient way to ingest nicotine in the chaos of the battlefield.[3]

The soldiers duly became addicted, and took the habit back to America with them. But the shortage of men had brought women into the workforce and thus public life, over something that invested the suddenly popular cigarettes with particular meanings.

Throughout the 1920s, those women, now accustomed to earning a living, associated cigarettes with their new independence. In response, conservatives railed against female smokers, identifying the habit with promiscuity and bohemianism. Vassar College and the University of California, neither of which had previously banned smoking, imposed anti-cigarette codes in 1925 and 1926 respectively, as the culture war intensified.[4] But they were fighting a losing battle. Between 1923 and 1929, the proportion of cigarettes smoked by women more than doubled.[5] In 1921, the women's editor of the student paper at Stanford nearly lost her job for suggesting that ladies might smoke. Only six years later, the university lifted the ban.[6]

The tobacco companies approached female consumers gingerly, torn between capitalising on a new market and offending the old moralists. After the First World War, for instance, the Lorillard company experimented with using fashionable women in its advertisements. But it did not dare show its models puffing cigarettes, or even holding them, instead merely positioning open packs suggestively in the foreground.

In 1926, Liggett & Meyers took another step, running ads showing a man smoking a Chesterfield while his partner looked on longingly.

'Blow some my way,' ran the caption.[7]

Two years later, George Washington Hill from the American Tobacco Company employed Edward Bernays, the pioneer PR guru (and nephew of Sigmund Freud) to popularise its Lucky Strikes brand with women.

Hill's initial efforts centred on nicotine's properties as an appetite suppressant. Under the slogan 'Reach for a Lucky instead of a sweet', Bernays enlisted 'expert' testimony to rebrand cigarettes. He convinced Dr George F Buchan, the former chief of the British

Association of Medical Officers of Health, to explain the relationship between sugar and tooth decay — and tell women to finish their meals with 'fruit, coffee, and a cigarette'. Bernays persuaded the editor of *House and Garden* to endorse menus saving women 'from the dangers of overeating' by advising the consumption of cigarettes instead of dessert, and he encouraged home economic writers to stress 'the importance of cigarettes in home-making'.[8]

By the end of 1928, Hill boasted that American Tobacco's revenue had grown by $32 million in a year, with Lucky Strikes showing 'a greater increase than all other cigarettes combined'.

Yet he wasn't satisfied. Women might light up at home, but most feared to be seen with a cigarette in public.

'How can we get women to smoke on the street?' Hill fretted.

Bernays devised a plan. He compiled a list of thirty debutantes, and sent them a telegram inviting them to 'fight another sex taboo … by smoking cigarettes while strolling on Fifth Avenue Easter Sunday'. He signed the message in the name of his secretary, Bertha Hunt — and then induced the prominent feminist Ruth Hale to publish a supportive statement in the newspapers.

Though every element of the ensuing Easter Parade was scripted, most journalists duly reported it as a spontaneous demonstration — perhaps not surprisingly, given that Hunt denied being connected with any company. 'I hope that we have started something,' she told the press, 'and that these torches of freedom … will smash the discriminatory taboo on cigarettes for women and that our sex will go on breaking down discriminations.'[9]

For the rest of his life, Bernays was celebrated (by himself and by others) as 'the father of PR', a role he often discussed in relation to his uncle's theories about the unconscious mind.

But how was that PR used?

In 1953, the presidents of American Tobacco, Benson and Hedges, Philip Morris, and US Tobacco met with the PR company

Hill & Knowlton in a fancy hotel in New York.

The previous year, *Readers Digest* — at the time, the most widely circulated publication in the world — had published an article under the headline 'Cancer by the carton'. The piece reported on evidence linking tobacco to tumours in mice. All through 1953, the press had been amplifying the story. The cigarette companies knew they faced an existential crisis. As the US Department of Justice later explained, they decided upon a concerted effort to 'deceive the American public about the health effects of smoking'.[10]

The campaign that followed built on the methods developed by Bernays. Just as he had deployed external 'experts' to persuade women to buy Lucky Strikes, John Hill from Hill & Knowlton devised a strategy whereby friendly scientists would cast doubt on the link between tobacco and cancer. In essence, they would engineer controversy where previously there had been none.

Hill & Knowlton compiled whatever statements they could find from experts that were even vaguely critical of existing research. They distributed the material to journalists and politicians, insisting they look at 'both sides of the story'.

That was merely the beginning.

'We should create a committee with "research" in the title,' a company document explained, 'so that the public recognise the existence of weighty scientific views which hold there is no proof that cigarette smoking is a cause of lung cancer.' In early 1954, the big cigarette-makers launched the Tobacco Industry Research Committee (TIRC), with an initial annual budget of $1.2 million and the support of twenty-three Hill & Knowlton employees.[11]

They announced this to the public in full-page advertisements in more than 400 newspapers, under the headline a 'Frank Statement to Cigarette Smokers'. The ads explained the industry's supposed concern for both science and its customers.

'We believe the products we make are not injurious to health,' it said. 'We always have *[sic]* and always will co-operate closely with those whose task it is to safeguard the public health'.[12]

Both sentences were lies.

Precisely because the TIRC tracked the science on smoking so assiduously, the industry realised that the link between cigarettes and cancer was robust. Its own program was not driven by an interest in health, but flowed from its public relations agenda. The TIRC distributed significant research funding, but did so under the auspices of a Scientific Advisory Board consisting of friendly scientists chosen by Hill & Knowlton. Rather than investigating the carcinogens in cigarettes, it challenged the basic science of cancer, funding scientists and studies it hoped might push the field in entirely different directions. As one historian put it, 'The TIRC was designed to direct attention away from the issue of immediate concern to the American public and American medicine: the health effects of smoking.'[13]

Rather than making consumers safer, the industry used its own research program to challenge each new study of tobacco, often issuing rebuttals before stunned scientists could even publicise their findings. The constant intervention by pro-cigarette 'researchers' created the perception of debate, transforming the health impacts of smoking from a medical issue into a controversy about which reasonable people could agree to disagree.

'From time to time, man-on-the-street interviews ask about the smoking question,' gloated Hill & Knowlton in 1962. 'In almost every one of these, there will be a quotation that is almost an exact paraphrase of some statement issued for the tobacco accounts.'[14]

Industry observers had expected cigarette consumption to decline through the 1950s once tobacco's health effects became known. That wasn't what occurred. Instead, because the 'cancer by the carton' stories spurred the industry's massive PR campaign, the new knowledge about the dangers of cigarettes led not to a decrease but a dramatic increase in smoking, as per capita cigarette consumption grew from 3,344 a year in 1954 to 4,025 in 1961.

That successful promotion of a harmful product provided a blueprint for other industries — most notably, for the fossil-fuel corporations as they confronted global warming.

Just as the cigarette companies knew what their products did to the human body, oil producers understood, from a remarkably early date, their effects on the climate.

In 1955, the American Petroleum Institute (API) financed research showing that the combustion of fossil fuels had led to an increase of atmospheric carbon by about 5 per cent. Two years later, Humble Oil — later better known as Exxon — commissioned a similar study. That same year, Edward Teller explained to oil and gas engineers that fossil fuels could engender climate change. In 1959, Teller spoke at an event hosted by the API and the Columbia Business School, and warned that carbon might warm the planet sufficiently that 'the icecaps ... start melting and the level of the oceans ... begin to rise'. In 1968, API research conducted by the Stanford Research Institute found that the continued consumption of fossil fuels would mean 'significant temperature changes' by the year 2000.[15] In 1978, Exxon researcher James Black produced an internal report that argued 'a doubling of carbon dioxide is estimated to be capable of increasing the average global temperature by from one degree to three degrees, with a ten-degree rise predicted at the poles'.[16]

In 1980, representatives from companies including Exxon, Texaco, and Shell agreed at an API meeting that one degree of warming was likely by 2005, that by 2038 the world would have warmed by 2.5 degrees, and that by 2067 the planet would face the 'globally catastrophic effects' of a five-degree increase.[17] In 1986, Shell produced a confidential company report that, while acknowledging uncertainties in climate predictions, warned of 'fast and dramatic' changes with 'major social, economic, and political consequences'.[18] Nothing, however, was done.

In 1991, Shell funded a film, *Climate of Concern*, which discussed the possibility of climate change 'too fast perhaps for life to adapt', with tropical islands submerged and 'greenhouse refugees' driven from their homes.[19]

It was never screened.

By the early 1990s, the fossil-fuel industry was using the same tactics as the tobacco companies — and, indeed, even the same people. Like the cigarette manufacturers, the oil producers sought out contrarian scientists to create an impression of controversy. Two of its most important experts were the physicists Frederick Seitz and Fred Singer, both of whom had played similar roles for the tobacco industry in its attempt to discredit medical research.[20]

The industry funded the Global Climate Coalition, which supported lobbying and PR, including the distribution of a video to journalists and politicians suggesting that because carbon dioxide helped crops grow, emissions could be a solution to world hunger.

Like the tobacco manufacturers before them, the oil companies demanded that the media present 'both sides of the story', insisting that the science remained unsolved. This was, of course, entirely cynical. While Exxon funded PR companies to discredit researchers, its own scientists discussed how the melting Arctic could 'help lower exploration and development costs for oil companies'.[21] Mobil Oil and Shell pumped money into disinformation — and yet redesigned their drilling platforms to take rising sea levels into account.[22]

Just as Big Tobacco succeeded in increasing smoking rates after 1953, the fossil-fuel industry managed to intensify emissions despite scientists' warnings. The vast majority of the carbon dioxide in the atmosphere today was released after (rather than before) the signing of the Kyoto Protocol. The global warming did not, in other words, result from simple ignorance. The fossil-fuel lobby understood full well what business as usual would mean — and deployed all their resources to make sure it happened.

It's tempting to describe as 'evil' the men and women who would act in such a way. Yet a purely moral judgement obscures a crucial aspect of the campaign that made climate change inevitable.

In his 1928 book *Propaganda*, Bernays explained the power of modern PR. Its techniques, he said, allow 'a relatively small number of persons ... who understand the mental processes and social patterns of the masses to pull the wires which control the public mind ... [to] harness old social forces and contrive new ways to bind and guide the world'.[23]

The description brings to mind the remarkable efforts of climate-change deniers to normalise the destruction of nature. But Bernays also argued that the 'propaganda' he described was not primarily a conspiracy, so much as an inevitable consequence of capitalist economics.

'In theory,' he said, 'everybody buys the best and cheapest commodities offered him on the market. In practice, if everyone went around pricing, and chemically testing before purchasing, the dozens of soaps or fabrics or brands of bread which are for sale, economic life would become hopelessly jammed.'[24]

PR arises, he claimed, as a necessary consequence of generalised competition between commodity owners. The struggle to find buyers makes advertising essential, as each business seeks to attract attention from others. As companies become larger, that process inevitably extends from a simple description of a product's virtue into more complicated attempts to reshape public sentiment.

Bernays' own career provides an illustration.

Lucky Strike cigarettes were known for their green packaging. Yet surveys showed that women disliked their cartons, since the unmodish hue clashed with their clothes. Having spent millions establishing the branding, Hill refused to change — leaving Bernays with a PR problem.

He responded by reshaping fashion. He convinced a society hostess to preside over a charity ball at the Waldorf-Astoria hotel, telling her that 'a nameless sponsor would defray the costs up to $25,000 ... [and] the color green would be the ball's motif and the obligatory color of all the gowns worn at the ball'.

He organised the Onondaga Silk Company to host a Green Fashions Fall luncheon, in which fashion editors were treated to an entirely green menu while an academic lectured on 'Green in the Work of Great Artists', a psychologist mused on the colour's unconscious significance, and representatives from the Color Fashion Bureau gave advice on how to make green work in the home.

'It looks like a Green Winter,' declared *The New York Sun* in the lead-up to the ball, while the *Post* celebrated a 'Green Autumn'. Clothing stores stocked their windows with green gowns, *Vogue* ran two pages on the green dresses coming from Paris, and the Color Fashion Bureau received requests for assistances from seventy-seven newspapers, ninety-five magazines, 301 department stores, 175 radio stations, and scores of manufacturers, decorators, and illustrators.

Suddenly, the packaging of Luckies became in vogue — and no one suspected American Tobacco's role.[25]

Organising a themed ball is not, of course, comparable to demobilising climate action. Yet, in Bernays' progression from publicising a brand to re-inventing fashion, we can see how even the most conspiratorial manifestations of PR arise from everyday economic forces. Capitalists must advertise their commodities; advertising involves manipulation; the scale of that manipulation spreads as corporations grow.

Competition meant that tobacco manufacturers were always going to target female smokers — for if one corporation didn't, its rivals would. To establish that market, they needed to reshape the public's ideas about the meaning of smoking and the status of women. By the 1950s, reshaping social attitudes was already part and parcel of what selling cigarettes involved, and so the companies were predisposed to see fears about cancer as merely another obstacle to overcome. The fossil-fuel industry made the same calculation, with climate denialism emerging from the deep structure of capitalism: not as a bug, but as a feature.

If we understand corporate PR not as a conspiracy, but as an outgrowth of economic logic, we're better able to grasp how and why it works.

For instance, until the Second World War, both retailers and their customers expected drink containers to be re-usable. But manufacturers recognised the potential of throw-away packaging, making disposable cans and bottles ubiquitous in the first phases of the Great Acceleration.

The environmental consequences became apparent very quickly. As early as 1953, farmers in Vermont were protesting about the rubbish accumulating in their fields — and, much to the horror of the manufacturers, the state legislature responded with a ban on disposable bottles.

In and of itself, the prohibition was trivial, a minor setback in a relatively small market. But the companies feared the precedent that even limited anti-pollution legislation represented. They did not, however, respond under their own names. Instead, the American Can Company, inventors of the single-use can, and the Owens-Illinois Glass Company, makers of disposable bottles, embarked on a Bernays-style campaign.

Alongside more than twenty other companies — including Coca-Cola, the Dixie Cup Company, the Richfield Oil Corporation, and the National Association of Manufacturers — they created a new organisation called Keep America Beautiful (KAB).[26] As its name suggested, KAB campaigned against pollution — but in a very specific fashion. In the same way that the auto lobby popularised the term 'jaywalker', KAB coined the new term 'litterbug' to describe those it held responsible for pollution. An American Can executive summed up its message in the phrase 'Packages don't litter, people do.' KAB distributed booklets and promotional flyers to schools and municipal bodies that blamed litterbugs for the packaging strewn throughout the landscape. It sought support from local communities and churches interested in beautification, and within a few years it was active in thirty-two states, with some 70 million members.

KAB combined its educational campaign with political lobbying for laws punishing individuals guilty of throwing away bottles and cans. Crucially, such measures were presented as a pro-business alternative to regulation of the industry. The Vermont law was thus defeated in 1957 by legislators instead intent on penalising litterbugs: the ordinary people supposedly to blame for the visible consequences of forced consumption. Throughout the 1960s, KAB screened TV advertisements in which a little girl called Susan Spotless scolded her parents for carelessly dropping trash, and then sang a song urging viewers not to be a litterbug.

'As Susan Spotless says,' explained the narrator, 'Keep America Beautiful — make it a family project!'[27]

As public concern about environmental degradation intensified, KAB adapted. Susan Spotless and her family duly gave way to KAB's most iconic campaign, the so-called Crying Indian TV commercial first screened in 1971.

The ad featured an actor named 'Iron Eyes Cody', dressed in Native American buckskin and paddling a bark canoe down a seemingly pristine river. As he progresses, rubbish in the water becomes increasingly evident, and the camera pans out to reveal an urban setting. The actor leaves the river and walks towards a busy freeway, only to be showered by fast-food wrappers hurled from the window of a passing automobile. A voiceover intones: 'Some people have a deep, abiding respect for the natural beauty that was once this country. And some people don't.' A zoom shows Iron Eyes Cody's face as a tear slowly trickles down his cheek.

The commercial cleverly appropriates both a burgeoning countercultural interest in Native American lifestyles and the new hostility to pollution associated with the social movements of the 1960s. Yet it fails to mention that KAB was a product of the big corporations — and neglects to explain that Iron Eyes Cody was actually an Italian–American man called Espera de Corti.

Moreover, despite the depiction of an industrial skyline, the message retains the same focus on individual responsibility, with a voiceover explaining: 'People start pollution. People can stop it.'[28]

Obviously, people can stop pollution. People do litter. They do consume the plastic containers and single-use bottles and polystyrene fast-food wrappers that despoil forests and lakes. They can make other choices.

But the circumstances in which such choices get made have been totally transformed by the practices of big business. Where shoppers might have replenished their stock of staples such as flour, coffee, or beans using their own receptacle, the shift to pre-packaged goods made sustainability inconvenient and, in many cases, impossible. In the post-war economy, the corporations increasingly replaced natural ingredients with synthetic detergents.[29] Consumers could decide between a dizzying array of products, but all of them came wrapped in single-use plastics.[30]

In fact, the same corporations that blamed ordinary Americans for the decisions they made continued to limit the options given to them to them. In 1972, Oregon and Vermont passed laws mandating a five cent deposit on beer and soft-drink containers: a modest scheme supposed to incentivise re-use. In 1974, California — a much larger market for drinks — debated a similar measure, KAB opposed the plan, with the group's president publicly testifying against the law. A few years later, proponents of bottle bills were denounced as 'communists' at a KAB board meeting.[31]

In reality, rather than promoting communism — or, for that matter, any collective solution — bottle bills actually encouraged individualised recycling, largely in keeping with KAB's message. But because mandated deposits cut into profits, the industry opposed them, irrespective of the environmental consequences.

The KAB story showed how effective corporate PR could be, particularly under certain conditions.

Obviously, like most third-party campaigns, KAB depended on deception. By the 1980s, it was receiving millions of dollars each year from 200 companies collectively responsible for one-third of the material ending up in American landfill. Few of the ordinary Americans who supported its work knew that KAB was funded by corporations that incinerated toxic waste, nor that its directors included representatives of Philip Morris, Mobil Chemical, Procter & Gamble, and PR giant Burson-Marsteller.[32]

But KAB was not merely a deception — or, more exactly, its deception worked because it reflected the logic of everyday capitalist life. Ordinary Americans found the despoliation of the environment genuinely distressing, and sought to do something about it. KAB could channel that sentiment into an argument about personal choice, a framework that made intuitive sense to people. Commodity exchange means that, most of the time, we relate to each other as independent economic units, making decisions about what we buy or don't buy. After all, capitalism always rests on 'choice'. We decide whether to buy one brand of toothpaste or another; we opt to work for one employer over another. It made sense to think we could simply choose to stop polluting.

Ironically, more or less exactly the same tactics that prevented recycling were later deployed to encourage recycling — and for similar reasons.

By the late 1980s, hostility to plastic was mounting. In 1989, with various legislatures considering bills to limit the material, Larry Thomas, the head of the Society of the Plastics Industry, summoned executives from Exxon, Chevron, Amoco, Dow, DuPont, Procter & Gamble, and other manufacturers to a crisis meeting at the Ritz Carlton.

'The image of plastics is deteriorating at an alarming rate,' he told them. 'We are approaching a point of no return.'[33]

The CEOs decided — of course! — on a PR campaign, with some $50 million a year to be pumped into advertisements about plastic recycling.

'The bottle may look empty, yet it's anything but trash … We've pioneered the country's largest, most comprehensive plastic recycling program to help plastic fill valuable uses and roles,' claimed a typical ad from 1990.[34]

With great fanfare, a series of environmental interventions were announced: ventures such as recycling centres, machines to sort plastics, and organisations dedicated to plastic recycling.

Yet, while plastic is very, very cheap to make from oil, it's very expensive to re-use. Predictably, most of the recycling projects closed within a few years. Meanwhile, industry lobbyists had surreptitiously persuaded some forty American states to include the recognisable recycling symbol (arrows in a form of a triangle) on plastic products. Well-meaning consumers duly dumped plastic trash into their recycling, where it contaminated the other waste.

Nevertheless, politicians, celebrities, and even many environmentalists urged the public to do their bit and recycle. We know now those efforts were almost entirely useless. The cheapness of new plastic undercut commercial recycling, so that most American waste was shipped to the developing world. Until a few years ago, China and Hong Kong purchased the bulk of that rubbish — and either burned or ploughed into landfill over 90 per cent of it. With the majority of American plastic too contaminated to re-use, best estimates put the percentage recycled at about 9 per cent.

In 2017, China banned the importation of plastic waste, in a campaign to clean up the toxic industry. Since then, American 'recyclers' have been sending shiploads to some of the poorest nations in the world — places such as Bangladesh, Laos, Ethiopia, and Senegal. A *Guardian* investigation described conditions prevailing in the Vietnamese village of Minh Khai, a centre of waste management where 'workers in makeshift workshops churn out recycled pellets amid toxic fumes and foul stench from the truckloads of scrap that are transported there every day'.[35]

The industry's success can be measured not simply by how, despite intensified opposition, it managed to massively intensify the use of plastic, but also in the way it pinned the blame on consumers. Recycling never offered a solution to the plastics crisis. Yet, by promoting recycling, the manufacturers and their lobbyists successfully displaced responsibility for pollution: if plastics clogged our rivers, seas, and landscapes, the fault lay with us, not them.

The same pattern occurred in respect of climate change. BP, one of the biggest oil companies in the world, initially responded to concern about warming by joining the Global Climate Coalition (GCC), a group that lobbied governments against action on greenhouse emissions. By 2001, with public awareness of the problem growing, it had withdrawn from the GCC and changed its name from British Petroleum to Beyond Petroleum. It then hired the PR firm Ogilvy & Mather for a publicity campaign that coined the notion of a 'carbon footprint'.

'What on earth is a carbon footprint?' one ad asked. 'Everybody in the world has one. It's the amount of carbon dioxide emitted each year due to the energy we use.' A handy calculator invited users to check their own footprint — and to learn about how BP was reducing its.[36]

Today, the term initiated by BP's campaign has become almost ubiquitous, a concept used by activists, by government agencies, and throughout the broader public. The US Environment Protection Agency urges Americans to check their carbon footprint, as do all manner of non-governmental organisations and lobby groups.

Yet, as BP well understands, the phrase mandates a particular logic, one that makes climate action almost impossible. By inviting the public to assess both their footprint and BP's, the campaign equates ordinary citizens with a giant corporation, implying an equality that simply doesn't exist. In other circumstances, the comparison would seem laughable — BP manages nearly 19,000 gas and oil stations worldwide. But the carbon footprint idea necessarily focuses an individual's attention on their own efforts, rather than BP's.[37]

More importantly, it sets the consumer a task that cannot possibly be achieved, encouraging actions that will make no appreciable difference. A study by MIT students showed that, if emissions from government and other services were divided equally among Americans, even homeless people, Buddhist monks, and infants scored twice as high as the world average.[38] No American could substantially reduce their carbon footprint, since carbon pollution was built into American society as a whole. You could sell your possessions and live under a cardboard box, and still your footprint would barely decline. The personal sacrifices called for in BP's advertising ('What size is your carbon footprint?') made no real difference to the environment and couldn't do so, as the corporation well understood. A campaign ostensibly urging awareness served instead to obscure the role played by companies such as BP, shifting the responsibility away from corporations and onto the public.

It's not, then, surprising that so many of us feel guilty about climate change and the environmental crisis, since we've been told for decades to do precisely that. The companies that urged ever greater consumption blamed us for the consequences. They gaslighted us into anti-pollution campaigns they recognised would not work, while they forestalled the solutions they knew existed.

Yet if we look more deeply into that appalling history, we can find definite reasons for optimism. The manufacturers hired PR firms to promote disposability precisely because they recognised that the public instinctively hated waste. If they channelled environmental sentiment into dead ends, they did so because they feared that sentiment would foster genuine change.

In other words, corporations understand something about ordinary people that escapes many environmentalists. They know the masses aren't innately greedy and selfish. It's well past time progressives accepted that, too.

CHAPTER EIGHT

The World's Worst Wound

'The lamps are going out all over Europe; we shall not see them lit again in our lifetime.' The comment that foreign secretary Sir Edward Grey supposedly made on the evening of 3 August 1914 referred to Britain's imminent entry into the First World War, a conflagration that brought the Edwardian era to a definite and bloody end. But the sentiment captures something of our own moment, amidst the steady ruination of the Earth.

'It may seem impossible to imagine,' writes Elizabeth Kolbert, 'that a technologically advanced society could choose, in essence, to destroy itself, but that is what we're now in the process of doing.'[1]

Kolbert delivered that assessment back in 2005, a lifetime ago in climate politics. In the years since, warnings from scientists have become more specific, shrill, and anguished — and yet the march to destruction has only quickened. '[T]here is a very big risk that we will just end our civilisation [if we continue on our present path]', warns professor Hans Joachim Schellnhuber from the Potsdam Institute for Climate Impact Research. '[W]e will destroy almost everything we have built up over the last two thousand years.'[2]

The extraordinary — almost absurd — contrast between how humanity is and should be responding fosters a particular kind of denialism. Experts might desperately publicise the diminution of Arctic ice, or the breakdown of ecosystems, or the proliferation of microplastics, but the political inaction blunts their message. *It can't be so bad*, we think, *or else something would be done. The rich and the powerful live on the planet, too. They're not going to stand aside while disaster consumes us all.*

That's why it's important to remember the Great War, a conflict that killed 20 million people and maimed 21 million others. War shattered the European economy, displaced entire populations, and set in motion events that culminated, scarcely two decades later, in even more apocalyptic slaughter. Yet, like climate change, it was a disaster foretold, a widely anticipated cataclysm that proceeded more or less on schedule, despite all the warnings about the horrors that lay ahead.

As early as 1898, Tsar Nicholas II of Russia initiated a conference to discuss international arbitration and to limit the arms race taking place in Europe. At its opening session at The Hague, he noted that the competition between nations, in which each country was building up its forces to defend against its neighbours, had 'transform[ed] the armed peace into a crushing burden that weighs on all nations and, if prolonged, will lead to the very cataclysm that it seeks to avert'.[3]

Over the next years, the rivalries intensified, leading to further militarisation and a complex series of (often secret) treaties, as, between 1908 and 1913, the military spending of the major powers increased by 50 per cent.

In early 1914, Winston Churchill noted that 'the world is arming as it has never armed before'. The eventual declaration of war in August came as a shock — but only in the sense that those attending a patient expiring from a long illness might still be startled by his death rattle.

Appeals to common humanity did not move states jostling for

trade and commercial advantages. For the people of Europe, the arms race was disastrous; for individual governments and specific business interests, it followed an unstoppable logic.

The same might be said of climate change.

To understand why, consider a puzzle that confronted James Maitland, the Earl of Lauderdale, in the early nineteenth century.[4] The earl noted that most people understood national wealth as the aggregated wealth of the citizenry. They assumed, logically enough, that if a person increased his fortune, the country would also be enriched, with the interests of the individual and the nation corresponding.

But, said Maitland, they could not be right.

To demonstrate, he invited readers to imagine a land suddenly having food in abundance. The nation would surely consider such plenty a blessing — and yet the surplus would impoverish those whose fortunes came from selling bread. Conversely, while only a madman would associate deprivation with an increase in the national wealth, an enforced drought would fill the coffers of those fortunate enough to possess a well.

Public wealth and private riches must, then, be different. The former, argued Lauderdale, consisted of 'all that man desires, as useful and delightful'. Private riches were also desired (otherwise why would anyone collect them?), but, unlike public wealth, they were defined by scarcity. Your riches were valuable precisely because they were hard to obtain. Breathable air belonged to the public wealth: it wasn't so much 'delightful' as utterly necessary. Nonetheless, oxygen couldn't enrich an individual — or, at least, it couldn't until it became scarce.

Even in Lauderdale's day, the paradoxical relationship between public and private interests could be identified. He noted that in Virginia, the favourable climate and rich soil produced tobacco in abundance. Yet commercial planters ensured the public did not benefit from the surplus by regularly destroying a certain proportion of the crop, thus creating an artificial shortage and boosting their profits.

The earl, scarcely a radical, found the implication that some people might gain by ruining everyone else both puzzling and alarming. Yet he couldn't disprove his own logic. 'So truly is this principle understood by those whose interest leads them to take advantage of it,' he wrote, 'that nothing but the impossibility of general combination protects the public wealth against the rapacity of private avarice.'[5]

The Lauderdale Paradox helps us to think about the incompatibility between personal and collective enrichment, and thus about the fundamental conflict between capitalism and nature. For Marx, Lauderdale's distinction between public wealth and private riches captures two different facets of value: use and exchange. Capitalism, he argued, mandates commodity circulation. It's a system in which we acquire our needs from the market rather than getting them made specifically. Every commodity must possess a use value: simply, someone, somewhere must want it, or it will remain unsold. But, for capitalists, the specifics of that don't matter. They measure value through exchange, making a quantitative assessment (via money) of each commodity against another. It's in this way they increase value.

The merchant does not buy crockery because she wants to set her own table. She doesn't care about use — she acquires her inventory to sell it for more than she paid. Likewise, if a factory churns out garden gnomes, it's not because its owner cares about landscape adornment, but because he can profit by selling the ornaments.

The nature of the system means that the satisfaction of needs takes place incidentally, in an accumulation driven by exchange rather than by use. The capitalist cannot make decisions primarily for the public good. She seeks profit — or else goes broke.

The distinction between use value and exchange value provides capitalism with its characteristic energy. Its dizzying technological achievements arise from a process that cannot rest, a circuit that must repeat and repeat and repeat. Capital means motion: a capitalist cannot hoard, but sends profits back into circulation to grow. The tools employed yesterday won't do today; the most modern methods become suddenly antiquated, as competition spurs businesses always to outdo each other.

But capitalist innovations are innovations for capital, ruled by the numerical assessments of value rather than by the interests of either humans or nature. The dominance of exchange allows a capitalist to transform a jungle into a desert, and then to relocate and continue working elsewhere. Her business isn't constrained by a particular ecosystem, but by the exigencies of profit, an abstraction removed from the specifics of people or land.

Capitalists aren't simply indifferent to the public good in their compulsion to chase exchange value. They're also unable to accept any limits, even those mandated by catastrophe. Other economic systems could tolerate constraints and work within boundaries. Capitalism cannot. If it doesn't grow, it dies. For capital, every obstacle serves only as a goad; each crisis, no matter how apocalyptic, provides the basis for renewed accumulation.

The First World War was widely expected because the commercial tensions between rival trade blocs had become so glaring and fraught. War emerged from the system's internal contradictions — and meant, in the short term, calamity for European capitalists. Hostilities closed every significant stock exchange on the continent. Many businesses struggled in wartime conditions; the fighting annihilated a huge chunk of economic infrastructure, leaving a considerable portion of Europe in ruins.

For capital, the Great War was a disaster. But it was also an opportunity, a chance to facilitate a restructuring from which further growth emerged. The war drew the most remote regions of the world into commodity circulation. It tore millions of people from the soil, and acclimatised them to wage labour. The extended supply lines of the battlefields created the international value chains of twentieth-century multinationals; dramatic technical improvements to weapons and equipment transformed entire industries.

In 1914, business ran on coal — but, by 1918, they'd reorganised to grow, running now on oil.

The same logic applies today.

In March 2019, marine biologist Darrell Blatchley and other scientists from the D'Bone Collector Museum in Davao City in the Philippines filmed themselves tugging plastic from the capacious digestive tract of a dead Cuvier's beaked whale. They eventually retrieved an astonishing forty kilograms of waste, including sixteen rice sacks, four banana plantation bags, and a huge quantity of disposable plastic.[6]

The viral circulation of the grotesque scene added to the woes of an industry facing renewed outrage about the spread of microplastics throughout the food chain. As legislators once again contemplated restrictions on packaging and other single-use plastics, the manufacturers pre-empted them. Dow Chemical, ExxonMobil, Henkel, Mitsui Chemicals, SABIC, Shell, and other major companies announced the formation of the Alliance to End Plastic Waste. This time, they said, they were serious, pointing to the billion dollars or so they'd collectively contributed to the new organisation. With that massive capital, they would, they said, prove the investment market of plastic waste to private investors, development banks, and governments to deliver 'truly transformational change'.[7]

On the Indonesian island of Bali, the alliance supported sustainable waste collection projects. In Accra in Ghana, it worked with female entrepreneurs to develop plastic-recycling businesses. It funded innovative high-tech sorting machines; it invested in chemical-recycling technologies and new ways of re-using plastic.

All were laudable endeavours — or, at least, they might have been, if they were intended to reduce the use of plastic. But they weren't. The Alliance to End Plastic Waste sought to end waste. It did not seek to end plastic. Rather, its member companies wanted to make more — much, much more — of the stuff. Their attempts to reduce the wastage associated with each unit of plastic corresponded with efforts to facilitate vastly increased production.

In 2019, when the new group launched, Shell was already planning a huge new plant in Pennsylvania (where shale gas would generate 1.6 million more tonnes of polyethylene); ExxonMobile was proceeding with a polyethylene production line in Texas (part of what would be one of the largest plastic factories in the world); and SABIC was launching a gigantic new oil-to-petrochemicals venture.[8] Since 2010, the member corporations of the alliance had collectively allocated more than $180 billion to new-generation plants, an investment predicated on a 40 per cent increase in plastic use over the following decade.[9]

Just as the tobacco industry responded to the health crisis of the 1950s by selling more cigarettes, and just as fossil-fuel companies reacted to climate change by increasing emissions, the plastic-makers used the new hostility to its product as an opportunity to re-organise and re-focus, with the Alliance to End Plastic Waste forging a path for expansion into the future.

This was not in any respect anomalous. It was simply good business sense. The best way to end plastic waste would be to cease making it, a decision obviously in the interest of the planet. But CEOs can't put the needs of the public ahead of their own bottom line, for fear of going broke.

Capitalism must grow. Its blind search for profit might bring disaster, but it will still sniff out opportunities for expansion, indifferent to experience or consequences. As a result, even measures that might alleviate the environmental crisis become immediately weaponised against the planet.

For instance, the panels that produce solar electricity have improved at a remarkable rate, offering a tantalising glimpse of a future powered by the sun's limitless power. The advances made in renewables and associated technologies (such as battery storage) will play a huge role in any serious response to the environmental crisis.

Yet researchers Richard York and Shannon Elizabeth Bell caution that capitalism has already undergone many previous energy transitions: from biofuels (such as wood) to coal, from coal to oil, from oil to natural gas, and now, potentially, from fossil fuels to renewables. They warn that no established energy source has undergone a sustained decline merely because a new one became available. More typically, rather than replacing the older source, the new source is immediately used to intensify growth and thus more overall energy use.

In many cases, the addition of new sources has actually increased consumption of previous types of energy. The embrace of fossil fuels led, in relative terms, to a decline in biofuels. Yet, in absolute terms, the use of petroleum in logging trucks and mills greatly intensified deforestation and thus produced a net increase in the use of wood. Similarly, the rise of petroleum did not curtail trade in whale oil, but instead fostered a dramatic intensification of whaling — partly because whale ships became much more efficient, and partly because the industry developed new uses (such as in margarine) for its products.[10]

It remains to be seen whether renewables will have the same effect. The available figures show a significant shift to renewable energy in terms of new capacity, with investment in renewables outpacing fossil fuels. Yet, internationally, the percentage of renewable energy as a proportion of electricity and other energy has been very slow to change.[11] Renewable-energy consumption has increased — but overall energy consumption has increased far, far more.

There's no mystery as to why.

In 1865, William Stanley Jevons published a book entitled *The Coal Question*. The titular query centred on Britain's response to the rapid depletion of its coal stocks, with the book most remembered today because of Jevons' rejection of claims that technologically driven energy efficiency would alleviate the shortage. 'It is wholly a confusion of ideas to suppose,' he said, 'that the economical use of fuel is equivalent to a diminished consumption. The very contrary is the truth.'[12]

What he meant was that efficiency decreases price and thus encourages use, leading to a rebound that wipes out the supposed savings. The so-called Jevons Paradox has been demonstrated over and over again in the years since. A prosaic example involves refrigerators, with the improvements of new models corresponding not to a decline in the overall environmental impact of whitegoods, but rather fostering a huge boom in the industry, and so a massive total rise in both energy consumption and carbon dioxide output.[13]

Because capital must expand, technologies that, in the abstract, should reduce resource use become the basis for a reorganisation that enables fresh accumulation. The first generation of computer users will remember the claim that the machines would make paper redundant — something that palpably failed to occur, as computerisation provided fresh markets supplying home and office printers. Likewise, the invention of synthetic alternatives did not mean that natural fibres were no longer required — instead, their production massively expanded in parallel with the new options.

Enthusiasts for 'green capitalism' insist that, as economies mature, their 'material footprint' — the measure of their environmental impact — declines. In the digital era, they say, technological progress decouples capitalist growth from ecological damage, allowing the system to expand safely into infinity.

Yet while some individual economies have reduced their dependence on non-renewable resources, they've generally done so by outsourcing dirty industries. As a meta-analysis of 179 studies between 1990 and 2019, put it, 'no evidence for the needed kind of decoupling currently exists'.[14] On the contrary, the materials used by the global economy have passed 100 billion tonnes per year — a disturbing new record, and the exact opposite of 'dematerialisation'.[15] '[N]ot only is there no empirical evidence supporting the existence of a decoupling of economic growth from environmental pressures on anywhere near the scale needed to deal with environmental breakdown,' explained a major 2019 report for the European Environmental Bureau, 'but also, and perhaps more importantly, such decoupling appears unlikely to happen in the future.'[16]

Think of electric vehicles — a mode of transport far less destructive than internal-combustion engines. Like solar power, EVs will surely play an important role in a sustainable future. Under capitalism, however, they've been seized upon by the automotive industry to preserve and extend car culture. Rather than reducing waste and decoupling transportation from material inputs, the automotive companies see opportunities to renew old markets in Europe and North America, and to open fresh ones in places such as China. Their success in selling high-tech private vehicles will, accordingly, forestall sustainable options such as bicycles and public transport, push cities to maintain the wasteful infrastructure designed around cars, and foster a new and ruinous race for lithium, cobalt, nickel, manganese, and other rare materials needed for batteries.

If the tendency of capitalism to respond to a crisis with more capitalism gives the system its disastrous momentum, it also provides the capitalists themselves with insulation from the consequences of their actions. The intensified commodification resulting from each fresh calamity creates opportunities for those with disposable wealth to ensure that they and their loved ones remain more or less unaffected. The planet might be growing unbearably hot, but if you have the money, you can still live in air-conditioned comfort in a pleasant location. In the midst of mass extinctions, luxury eco-resorts and private zoos allow the well-to-do to gaze on tigers and orangutans and elephants.

That's why, even a looming apocalypse will not, in and of itself, motivate a change of course.

It's symptomatic that a burgeoning mini-industry now caters to plutocrats seeking a base on the unpolluted and remote South Island of New Zealand, where they, their families, and (perhaps) their friends might shelter as the world collapses. The Texas-based Rising S Company — 'we don't sell fear, we sell preparedness' — claims to have constructed at least ten private bunkers in the country in the last few years, with a low-end shelter of 150 tons costing the owner about $3 million or so. The rival Vivos corporation boasts that a facility it installed north of Christchurch provides for some 300 people in appropriate comfort.[17]

The same logic prevails among a billionaire CEO class increasingly preoccupied with interplanetary escape. At Space X, Elon Musk intends to establish a colony on Mars, populated by pioneers paying $500,000 for a one-way trip; the Blue Origin project of Amazon's Jeff Bezos prefers to send them to the Moon.[18]

A few, even more ambitious, members of the One per cent plan to escape the material world altogether. Google's Ray Kurzweill, for instance, expects nano-robots to soon provide 'full immersion virtual reality from within the nervous system and will connect our neocortex to the cloud'.[19] Start-up accelerator Y Combinator already offers a process called 'aldehyde-stabilised cryopreservation', a method by which a human brain can be 'vitrified' (that is, turned to glass) preparatory to its eventual transfer (through a technology as yet undeveloped) into digital storage. As a result, an entrepreneur might live forever as ones and zeros, liberated from nature's ongoing decline.

One might dismiss these and other plans to avoid the palpably encroaching environmental disasters as childish fantasies, akin to those that most of us grow out of during our teenage years. But that would miss the point. Billionaire survivalism is better understood as the extreme extension of the more prosaic methods by which the wealthy and privileged evade the crises that everyone else must endure. Most capitalists won't blast off to Mars. They will, however, flee from the most polluted zones to maintain privileged lives while the destruction they oversee runs its course.

Siegfried Sassoon called the Great War the 'world's worst wound'. The description sounds almost naïve, given what the planet has endured since. But as Sassoon's generation learned, the unthinkable can all too easily be normalised — unless we actively stop it.

CHAPTER NINE

The Great Race

In May 2020, a video circulated of an aggrieved white woman in New York's Central Park threatening to summon the police after Christian Cooper, an African-American birdwatcher, asked her to leash her dog. In the wake of the Black Lives Matter protests, she knew full well what the arrival of armed officers might mean for his safety.

In the interviews he gave later, Cooper related the incident to a broader hostility that African-Americans experienced in the birdwatching community, where they were persistently treated as unwelcome outsiders.

In support of Cooper, the ecology professor J Drew Lanham subsequently published an article entitled 'Nine New Revelations for the Black American Birdwatcher'. 'You'll need the binoculars to pick that tufted duck out of the flock of scaup and ring-necks,' he wrote. 'You'll need the photo ID to convince the cops, FBI, Homeland Security, and the flashlight-toting security guard that you're not a terrorist or escaped convict.'[1]

As Lanham implies, birding provides no escape from racism. On the contrary, for many African-Americans, the outdoors invokes bigotry, the Klan, and racial violence. The woods, they say, is where black people go — and then don't ever come back from.[2]

In part, this perception stems from a geographical shift in the early twentieth century, a time when the Great Migration took African-Americans out of rural oppression in the south to better-paying jobs in the industrialised cities of the north. But the association of nature with whiteness also derives from developments within environmentalism itself. That is, many of the most influential ecological pioneers in the United States espoused a virulent racism and elitism — a bigotry not incidental to their ecology, but deeply entwined with it, in ways that have continuing implications for the fight against climate change.

When the French aristocrat and political philosopher Alexis de Tocqueville voyaged to America in 1832, he pondered on how the colonists regarded the land they had occupied. Europeans, he said, marvelled at the natural beauty of the country, but the Americans themselves didn't share their awe. The settlers barely noticed the forests they levelled or the plains over which they tramped. Instead, the Frenchman said, they saw only their own march across the wilds, with the landscape merely a backdrop to their self-regard as magnificent conquerors of nature.[3]

Furthermore, because the American 'wilds' already contained millions of human beings, the settler conceptions of nature always possessed a racial dimension, a connection forged even before the colonists landed.[4] For the European arrivals, the conquest of the land meant the conquest of Indigenous people, who were, as we've seen, themselves understood as part of the natural world. The enslavement of African-Americans both rested on and reinforced a similar mentality, with planters treating their slaves as mere aspects of production, of the same order as the cotton they harvested and the soil they tilled.

In Europe, industrialisation inspired a counter-perspective — one that, in many ways, simply reversed the old polarities. The writers, artists, and thinkers we call the Romantics understood the smokestacks and slag heaps of the new cities as stultifying rather than noble. The factory floor degraded men, they thought, crippling their capabilities and stunting their aspirations. The Romantics didn't celebrate civilisation, but decried it; they revelled instead in a spirituality associated with nature in extremis — a celebration of jagged mountains and storms and wild rivers.

In America, the sentiment took a different form.[5] In 1890, the superintendent managing the official census realised that he could no longer identify a clear line of advancing settlement. The frontier, he declared, had ended. That dramatic announcement — in essence, a recognition of colonisation's completion — spurred widespread nostalgia and a so-called Wilderness Cult, a mass enthusiasm for trekking, mountain climbing, hunting, and other outdoor pursuits.

The young Theodore Roosevelt was a particularly keen cultist. In 1887, he called together a meeting of aficionados of the 'manly sport with the rifle' — that is, big-game hunting. Symptomatically, Roosevelt's Boone and Crockett (B&C) Club took its name from, as Roosevelt put it, 'two typical pioneer hunters'.[6] But, precisely because the frontier no longer existed, the animals that the clubmen most liked to hunt were becoming harder to locate, having been dispersed or even eliminated by the spread of European settlement. If Roosevelt and his friends wanted to kill game, they realised, they would need to preserve it.

From this unlikely, paradoxical effort to save animals so they could be shot came one of America's first sustained campaigns for 'conservation' — a term that, symptomatically, B&C founding member George Bird Grinnell coined. By 1902, the club included not only several more or less full-time conservationists, but also a significant cross section of the American elite, including businessmen, philanthropists, members of the House of Representatives, senators, the secretary of war, the man who would become secretary of state, and, in Roosevelt, a future president of the United States.[7]

Still in existence today, the B&C Club helped create and expand many of the major American national parks, led and organised almost all the important early conservation groups, and lobbied for, supported, and publicised the most significant early environmental legislation, including the Lacey Act, the Reclamation Act, the National Wildlife Refuge System Act, the Migratory Bird Act, the Migratory Bird Hunting Stamp Act, and the Pittman-Robertson Act.[8] During his presidency, Roosevelt drew on his friends at the B&C almost as a brains trust for issues relating to nature, so much so that some claimed that the ideas of the group became national policy.[9]

Unfortunately, those ideas extended from the natural world to the social one, in several disastrous ways. Roosevelt believed that concepts developed from wildlife management could also be applied to humans. As a hunter, he feared the displacement or 'mongrelisation' of native species; as a president, he fretted about the 'the white race' giving way to the Irish, the Italians, or the Jews. Conservation, he explained, meant 'leaving this land even a better land for our descendants than it is for us, and training them into a better race to inhabit the land and pass it on'.[10]

It was a perspective widely shared throughout the B&C Club, as well as by the Sierra Club, the Sempervirens Club, the Save the Redwood Leagues, and many other early environmentalist bodies. Symptomatically, Gifford Pinchot, the Roosevelt-appointed first chief of the forest service, and another pioneer of the movement, simultaneously advised the American Eugenics Society. In that capacity, he urged Americans to back 'conservation in all its branches — but above all, the conservation of the racial stock itself'.[11] A similar sentiment prevailed at the National Conservation Congresses, an important Pinchot-initiated environmental measure. At the second-such event, Julia Scott, a representative of the Daughters of the American Revolution, implored attendees not only to treasure native flora and fauna, but to also conserve 'the supremacy of the Caucasian race in our land'.[12]

Perhaps most notoriously, Madison Grant, whom Roosevelt considered a 'particularly good fellow', popularised a bogus form of racial science across America and the world. Grant served as president of the New York Zoological Society; he also led the Eugenics Research Association and the Immigration Restriction League. He campaigned for the racist Emergency Quota Act of 1921 and the Immigration Restriction Act of 1924 — measures intended to exclude Jews, Asians, and other 'undesirables'.

Grant's 1916 book, *The Passing of the Great Race, or The Racial Basis of European History*, achieved huge popularity in America and, later, Germany. In it, he argued that the heritage of his country's 'pure Nordic stock' had come under threat from 'the weak, the broken, and the mentally crippled of all races drawn from the lowest stratum of the Mediterranean basin and the Balkans, together with hordes of the wretched, submerged populations of the Polish Ghettos'.[13] To preserve its racial character, America should legalise birth control, reduce 'the undesirable classes' through mass sterilisation, and implement segregation and anti-miscegenation laws.

Hitler famously described *The Passing of the Great Race* as his personal 'bible', and his own *Mein Kampf* contains many passages that Grant's biographer Jonathan Peter Spiro describes as inspired by 'Grantian thought'. During the Nuremberg trials, Major-General Karl Brandt of the Waffen-SS (Hitler's personal doctor and a key medical authority in the Nazi regime) sought (unsuccessfully) to defend himself by introducing as evidence excerpts from Grant's book, as well as details about the Immigration Restriction Act, American sterilisation programs, and anti-miscegenation legislation (all of which Grant had advocated).[14]

Understandably (and appropriately), Grant's record as a racist today overshadows his record as a conservationist. Yet his environmental achievements were undeniably extraordinary. Grant campaigned for the Bronx River Parkway, and helped create Glacier National Park and Denali National Park. His determination almost singlehandedly saved the bison, the populations of which had dropped from perhaps 60 million to 541 animals in 1889. He played a similar role in preserving the bald eagle, the pronghorn antelope, the Alaskan bear, and the fur seal, and his biographer also suggests he contributed to rescuing 'the elephants of Africa, the koalas of Australia, the chinchillas of South America, the gorillas of the Congo, the giant tortoises of the Galapagos Islands, the ibex of Spain, the mountain zebras of South Africa, the elephant seals of Mexico, the giant sable antelopes of Angola, the nyalas of Ethiopia, the white rhinos of the Sudan, the wisents of Poland, and several species of whales'.[15]

It would be comforting to draw a line between the man's racism and his conservationism, separating entirely the hateful ideas that Grant espoused from his stalwart defence of the natural world. It's more accurate and confronting to recognise their shared source.

The Romantic challenge to the older, unabashed hostility to nature treated otherness as a kind of mystical tonic. Ralph Waldo Emerson wrote of wilderness as a spiritual practice; Henry David Thoreau celebrated the woods and the fields and the lakes as redeeming a humanity harried by modernity. Thoreau's famous belief in 'wildness' as the 'preservation of the world' helped inspire America's first national parks, in accord with his belief that each town should establish 'a park, or rather a primitive forest, where a stick should never be cut for fuel, a common possession forever, for instruction and recreation'.[16] Yosemite Valley became such a place in 1864, and then Yellowstone in 1872, with imitative projects following across America and elsewhere.

By definition, the celebration of wilderness as untouched by humanity wilfully dismissed the Native American presence. When

John Muir — one of Thoreau's disciples — wrote about Yosemite, he celebrated the fact that 'no foot seems to have neared it' — in a diary entry written at almost precisely the place where US troops had captured the Native American leader Tenaya. Likewise, conservationists could champion Yellowstone's 'primeval solitude' only by ignoring the manifold trails criss-crossing the area.

Native Americans did not merely visit Yellowstone. They relied upon the land for food and shelter and the other basic interactions with nature on which human beings have always depended. Like Indigenous people in Australia, they sometimes lit fires, using flames to rejuvenate the soil and to help in hunting. The white authorities saw these blazes, not as a core element of the Native American economy, but as senseless vandalism. In response, the pioneer geologist John Wesley Powell argued that the state could only protect the forests of the American west from fires set 'in the main … by Indians' if it secured 'the removal of the Indians'.[17]

The emerging concepts of environmentalism duly provided another justification for the establishment of Native American reservations. If the migratory tribes could be forcibly constrained in specific locations, they would, of necessity, embrace European agriculture. As small farmers, they'd give up their warlike habits and assimilate, relying, like their white neighbours, on farming particular strips of land, and so leave the 'wilderness' free from human interference.

That argument bolstered the case for a program already in train. Authorities made the decision to declare Yellowstone a park in 1872, at the height of the enthusiasm for reservations, with the Blackfeet, Crow, Bannock, and Shoshone being confined to small areas in Montana, Wyoming, and Idaho.[18] Thereafter, the supporters of Yellowstone waged a continuing campaign against what Grinnell's *Forest and Stream* magazine called the 'bands of roaming savages' who tried to maintain their customary usages of the area. Roosevelt declared that Native Americans, unless curbed, would 'waste and destroy' Yellowstone; the Boone and Crockett Club passed a resolution calling for the government to prevent the 'destruction of forests and game' caused by traditional hunters.

The clubmen eventually got their wish. In 1886, cavalry from Fort Custer marched into the park and remained in occupation for the next thirty-two years. Many of those troops were veterans of the Indian wars; they set about securing Yellowstone using the tactics they'd developed during more conventional bouts of 'Indian fighting'.

As in Australia, the suppression of traditional land management produced disastrous ecological consequences. Several species of trees in Yellowstone depended on fire for their reproduction and so died away; others proliferated in areas that had previously been grasslands.

From the perspective of Native Americans, a form of conservation enforced by the same military that herded them into reservations merely changed the label under which their dispossession was consolidated. To local tribes, the preservationist rhetoric of Roosevelt and his friends could not be separated from the broader efforts by settlers to erase all traces of Indigenous culture, to consolidate the same power over Native American peoples that they exerted over the land itself.[19]

That relationship between early conservationism and the state reflected the social perspectives of the first wilderness campaigners. The B&C Club deliberately sought to organise an elite: those Grinnell called 'men of social standing', the rich individuals whose opinion he considered 'worth regarding'. Membership was limited to one hundred, with would-be applicants assessed on whether they'd successfully shot large game animals from at least three American species.[20]

The clubmen had made their money in the capitalist economies of the rising cities, which they saw as counterposed to the 'wilderness', identified with recreation. Interestingly, that also motivated their hostility to a certain class of whites.

The spread of the frontier had, after all, allowed settlers to establish households, and even communities, in remote areas, where they supported themselves through hunting and small-scale farming. Their lives, in many ways, mimicked the routines of pre-capitalist Europe, with their relationship with nature governed less by what they could sell than by the dictates of custom and mutually agreed codes.

Accordingly, these white rural communities also experienced the conservationist enthusiasm for wilderness as a form of externally driven modernisation, a process in which the state and its representatives imposed laws at odds with the locals' moral economy. In Yellowstone, for instance, the army's operations were directed as much at white 'poachers' as Native American hunters, with troops hunting down the trappers making a living from hunting game. Indeed, the class dynamic of the early movement manifested itself in the opposition of the B&C sportsmen to what they called 'pot hunting': basically, shooting for food or profit. For big-game shooters, the pot hunter — almost by definition, someone from the working class or the rural poor — was, in the words of an early hunting manual, 'the most disgusting, the most selfish, the most unmanly, the most heartless' character that 'a well-bred sportsman' might encounter.[21]

The club's campaigns against 'pot hunting' were explicitly racist. Earlier in the nineteenth century, the bulk of European settlers originated from Britain, Germany, or Scandinavia. But, between 1880 and 1924, some 25 million people made their way to America from southern, central, and eastern Europe. Many of them came from poor and rural backgrounds, in which ordinary people still relied directly on nature for sustenance. In America, they scandalised the respectable classes by trapping songbirds and cooking game that the locals didn't normally eat. In his book *Our*

Vanishing Wild Life, the B&C stalwart William Temple Hornaday
hailed 'gentlemen sportsmen' (like himself and his friends) as 'the
very bone and sinew of wild life preservation' — and then warned
against the Italians 'pouring into America into a steady stream' as
liable to 'quickly exterminate every wild thing that wears feathers or
hair'.[22] Such demonisations of immigrants in general, and Italians in
particular, dominated the early movement.

By the latter part of the nineteenth century, the remnants of
pre-capitalist attitudes to nature were being reshaped by capital
accumulation. In Yellowstone, the Native Americans and white
poachers who still hunted in the park did so not to feed themselves
and their families, but to sell hides and furs on the market, which
meant slaughtering animals on an entirely unsustainable basis. Men
and women who, in the Old World, supplemented their vegetables
with occasional meat from game now killed or captured birds in
commercial quantities. The measures for which the B&C Club
agitated (such as licensing schemes; prohibitions on traps and other
mechanisms; and restrictions on harvesting times) thus certainly
saved endangered creatures from extinction. But it also meant that
conservation, in practice, consisted largely of restrictions imposed
on poor people — and, in particular, poor people who were not
white — so as to control or reshape their interactions with nature.[23]

The B&C members did not, after all, oppose hunting or fishing
so much as oppose hunting or fishing as performed in certain ways.
Killing big-game species for pleasure was, they said, noble, manly,
and wholesome, but it was shameful, effeminate, and degenerate
to shoot the same animals for food or for money. Attitudes to the
wild thus came to signify particular attitudes to society. By the early
1900s, the authorities had added 'nature study' to the curriculum of
many public schools, on the basis that engaging in fresh-air outings
and country trips would help assimilate the urban poor into the
American project.[24]

The wilderness cult thus provided ideological support for the political right. If 'wildness' represented the preservation of the world, what did that mean for those who wouldn't or couldn't engage in manly outdoor sports? What did it tell you about the teeming masses who understand nature in the wrong way? Thoreau's gentle rhetoric could become a weapon against those who embodied contemporary degeneration: immigrants, 'lesser races', and the populace as a whole. A conservative tradition within European (and particularly German) Romanticism had long enlisted the natural world behind racialised nationalism. The philosopher Ludwig Klages, for instance, developed the idea of 'biocentrism' while blaming deforestation on modernity and Jews. Ernst Haeckel coined the term 'ecology' while developing a hierarchy of racial types (particularly admired by Grant).[25] Later, national socialist ideologues such as Richard Walther Darré popularised the slogan 'Blood and Soil', positing the German landscape as central to a semi-mystical nationalism that justified expansionism by the need for *lebensraum* (living space).

Grant simply took such arguments further, considering the liberal idea of America as 'the great Melting Pot where all the races of Europe are melting and re-forming'[26] as precisely the biological dilution that conservationists should prevent. In its obituary for Grant, *The New York Times* explained how 'the preservation of the redwoods, of the bison, of the Alaskan caribou, of the bald eagle … of the spirit of the early American colonist … and of the purity of the "Nordic" type of humanity in this country, were all his personal concerns, all products of the same urge in him to save precious things'.[27] In that passage, we can see not only Grant's racism, but the elitism underlying his entire project, a sentiment that could easily manifest as hostility to the population as a whole.

The sentiments expressed in *The Passing of the Great Race* were largely discredited by the Second World War and the horrific experience of Nazism. Brandt might not have been saved from the gallows by his testimony, but the parallels his lawyers made between national socialism and American thought rendered environmental eugenics increasingly toxic in the public sphere.

The early history of American environmentalism can make for bleak reading. Yet understanding the centrality of racism to the pioneer ecologists matters, and not simply because it allows a long-overdue moral reckoning with the forces that prevent an African-American man from enjoying the birds of Central Park. Too often, environmentalism has failed to inspire the people most affected by the destruction of the natural world, with the taint from Grant and his ilk still lingering. The enormous challenge of climate change mandates the broadest possible campaign — and that requires not just participation, but leadership from the oppressed and the excluded.

CHAPTER TEN

People, People, People

In 1798, the Reverend Thomas Malthus published *An Essay on the Principle of Population*, a tract he substantially re-worked in 1803. Famously, Malthus asserted that human populations expanded geometrically, while their food supplies only increased arithmetically. As a result, societies grew inexorably until they reached the limit of the resources available to them, at which point either people ceased having children, or famine and disease culled their ranks.

Malthus was not an environmentalist. In his schema, the problem wasn't natural shortages, but the tendency for human fertility to exceed any limits. For Malthus, any society, under any circumstances, kept increasing until hunger prevented its growth. Even the smallest group of people was thus, in his theory, teetering on the edge of overpopulation.

Malthus wasn't interested in deforestation or extinctions. He wrote to combat early measures for what we'd now call social security, insisting that his 'principle of population' proved the amelioration of poverty to be both impossible and undesirable. Welfare, he said, encouraged the destitute to raise dependents, swelling their numbers so that the rapacious poor consumed whatever new provisions they had been granted. Assisting the starving was not only ineffective but dangerous, something that risked the ruination of all.

In a passage from the second edition of his essay, Malthus explained how anyone who could neither find a job nor rely on relatives 'has no claim of right to the smallest portion of food'. Nature, he said, would quickly and rightfully punish such a fellow — by, presumably, starving him to death — unless soft-hearted philanthropists interceded. In that case, the well-meaning naïfs would cause more trouble than they averted, since the minute they aided one mendicant, others would immediately call upon them for help. The arrival of these new moochers would inevitably overwhelm even the best-provisioned do-gooder, transforming prosperity into generalised want, and creating a 'spectacle of misery and dependence', all because of what Malthus called 'the clamorous importunity of those who are justly enraged at not finding the provision which they had been taught to expect'.[1]

The reverend later felt obliged to remove that section of his text, precisely because its more or less explicit enthusiasm for famine so starkly revealed the central political function of the argument as a whole: namely, the justification of poverty as a biological necessity.

Nevertheless, despite such backpedalling, Malthus remained widely loathed by working people. In the 1830s, a scurrilous pamphlet by someone called 'Marcus' satirically extended Malthus's ideas into a proposal to exterminate the infants of England by gas — an idea much discussed in the Chartist press as the logical development of Malthusianism.[2]

But it wasn't just labour radicals who saw the reverend as despicable and inhuman. 'I have,' wrote the journalist and politician William Cobbett in an open letter to Malthus, 'during my life, detested many men; but never any one so much as you.'[3]

How did such an odious figure become associated with environmentalism?

Modern environmentalism burst into the awareness of

mainstream America on the first Earth Day in 1970. Perhaps 20 million Americans — an astonishing 10 per cent of the population — attended some kind of Earth Day event. The occasion attracted far more people than any of the anti-war protests or the civil rights marches. Some 1,500 colleges held teach-ins, alongside 10,000 schools. Earth Day enjoyed saturation coverage in newspapers and magazines. On TV, NBC devoted an entire week to the environment, while both *Sesame Street* and *Mister Rogers' Neighborhood* presented environmentally themed shows. One estimate put the number of speakers — those who addressed the crowds, rather than those who simply came to events — at perhaps 35,000. Many went on to become environmental organisers, with Earth Day helping to create a generation of activists.[4]

In retrospect, an interest in the well-being of the planet can be seen growing slowly during the post-war decades, manifesting in a resurgent liberalism, the student movement, and the preoccupations of women's liberation. Many historians point, in particular, to the success of Rachel Carson's *Silent Spring* as foreshadowing the new concern for nature and opposition to pollution.[5]

Nevertheless, the enthusiasm manifested on Earth Day also reflected the influence of Malthus — or, at least, Malthusianism.

Earth Day was initiated by senator Gaylord Nelson of Wisconsin. For Nelson, environmentalism meant responding to the growing numbers of people in America and the world. As he told a constituent in 1970, 'I have not given a speech on the environment in the last half dozen years in which I have not emphasised the disastrous consequences of the increasing population.'[6] Nelson took his sense of those 'disastrous consequences' from, in particular, Paul Ehrlich and his neo-Malthusian book *The Population Bomb*.

The precipitous decline in Ehrlich's reputation in recent years hides the influence he once wielded. *The Population Bomb* sold an astonishing 2 million copies, with its author one of the most recognisable public commentators of the era. At a time when few environmentalists could command a mass audience, Ehrlich appeared on Johnny Carson's *Tonight Show* a remarkable twenty times.[7]

His ideas — which we might describe as 'populationist' — permeated every aspect of Earth Day. A press release issued for the event decried the 'environmental problems being created by our advancing technology and expanding world populations'. Two weeks before Earth Day, Nelson explained that population growth constituted 'the world's biggest problem'. During the teach-ins, speaker after speaker denounced overpopulation. At Indiana University, for instance, a group threw birth-control pills into the crowd; elsewhere, students highlighted the famines that they said a growing population would bring by serving up a 'hunger diet' of tea and rice.[8]

The resurgence of populationist theories in post-war America might seem odd, given that tremendous economic growth diminished absolute deprivation in ways that Malthus never could have imagined. By 1945, far more people possessed far more wealth, an outcome entirely at odds with the reverend's contention that provision for the poor represented an unsustainable crime against nature. Nevertheless, the Cold War had drawn attention to those developing countries known collectively as the Third World, and, with the United States and the Soviet Union locked in stalemate, poorer nations became the frontline in struggles fought by proxy. In the American discussion of such places, populationism appealed precisely as it did in the early nineteenth century, by offering a biological explanation of mass poverty.

In 1954, the millionaire Hugh Moore published the first best-selling tract entitled *The Population Bomb*, a pamphlet that correlated rising birth rates with support of communism. A metaphorical explosion of fertility would, he said, culminate in a literal explosion of Red bombs, as the starving multitudes aligned with the Russians against the free world. Five years later, president Eisenhower presented a version of the same claim, worrying that the real threat faced by America came from 'the one and a half billion hungry people in the world'.[9] Anxiety over population growth in developing nations remained a staple of American foreign policy throughout the 1960s.

The rise of a more overtly environmentalist populationism was not unrelated. In 1948, William Vogt published a book called *Road to Survival*, and Fairfield Osborn released *Our Plundered Planet*. Both books repacked Malthus's tract into a more palatable argument about resource shortages. '[T]he earth is not made of rubber,' Vogt explained, 'it cannot be stretched; the human race, every nation, is limited in the number of acres it possesses.'[10] Accordingly, as the number of human beings increased, he argued, the relative amount of productive land must decrease.

Such books helped to establish a new intellectual framework for conservationists, one emphasising the relation between consumption and population growth. By 1959, the Sierra Club was imploring America to give overpopulation 'urgent attention'. In 1962, the naturalist Joseph Wood Krutch urged conservationists to 'face the fact that behind almost every problem of today lies the problem of population'.[11] Then, in 1968, the biologist Paul Ehrlich borrowed Hugh Moore's title for his own book.

Where Osborn and Vogt had been urgent, Ehrlich was verging on apocalyptic. 'The battle to feed all of humanity is over,' he declared. His book predicted an imminent mass famine, with global starvation one of many symptoms of a broader ecological and social crisis:

Too many cars, too many factories, too much detergent, too much pesticide, multiplying contrails, inadequate sewage treatment plants, too little water, too much carbon dioxide — all can be traced easily to too many people.[12]

By 1972, the Zero Population Growth group — formed as a direct result of Ehrlich's book — claimed 35,000 members.[13]

Throughout the 1970s, a string of publications — including Garrett Hardin's famous 'Tragedy of the Commons' essay, the 1972 Club of Rome publication *The Limits to Growth*, and the 1974 Rockefeller Commission's report on population control — kept populationism central to environmental thinking.

These publications stood against the tide of the intensified consumption of the post-war economy, at a time when politicians and the media linked prosperity directly and enthusiastically to the birth rate. 'Babies equal boom,' announced *Reader's Digest* in 1951, in a story stressing the importance of people for creating economic demand. In 1958, *Life* magazine featured a cover story describing children as a 'built-in recession cure', while signs in the New York subway flatly equated demographic and economic growth. 'Every day, 11,000 babies are born in America,' they declared. 'This means new businesses, new jobs, new opportunities.'[14]

While economists and advertisers called for more people to consume more, Ehrlich and others stressed what was being depleted, and then attributed that depletion to population growth. In 1917, Americans numbered 100 million; in 1967, the figure had ballooned to 200 million. As ordinary people saw the suburban sprawl eating up fields and forests, demography provided an intuitive explanation for what was taking place.

The need for birth control was, Ehrlich told them, imposed by physical reality. If the population continued to double, in 900 years one hundred people would crowd into every square yard of land and sea on the planet. After that, it would take only 'about 50 years to populate Venus, Mercury, Mars, the moon, and the moons of Jupiter and Saturn to the same population density', and another two centuries to overwhelm outer planets such as Jupiter and Uranus. Every new baby demanded food, shelter, clothing, and other resources — and each year there were more of them. The population would, inevitably, outstrip society's ability to provide, rapidly exacerbating all the social evils already menacing Americans.

'From rubbish to riots to starvation,' explained Ehrlich, 'we are faced with an array of problems, all of which can be traced, at least in part, to too many people.'[15]

The book's strident message suited strident times, offering a common-sense explanation for a society that, for many, felt entirely out of control. Liberals who loathed the tacky consumerism of the Great Acceleration, who anguished about Third World poverty, and feared the turmoil in America's ghettoes found Ehrlich's calls for restraint, better sexual education, more contraception, and tax incentives for childless families to be eminently reasonable. Even progressives could agree with the populationist critique of 'the capitalistic system' as, in Vogt's words, 'ruinous' because of its inexorable depletion of natural resources.[16]

Yet Ehrlich himself expressed little hope about short-term solutions. Furthermore, many of the proposals he did advocate were deeply illiberal. It was, he told one interviewer, 'highly unlikely that we will get through the next two decades without a major disaster resulting in the deaths of hundreds of millions of human beings'.[17] In the context of that apocalyptic prospect, Ehrlich resorted to the metaphor of disease to describe excess populations, urging governments to cease worrying about symptoms, but instead 'cut … out the cancer' — an operation that would, he said, 'demand many apparently brutal and heartless decisions'.[18]

That brutality was, by and large, intended for the developing world. Ehrlich suggested, for instance, that the United States 'train … paramedical personnel to do vasectomies' as part of a program of compulsory sterilisation for Indian men with three or more children.[19] Fortunately, Washington did not warm to the idea, but Indian prime minister Indira Gandhi did, in 1975, adopt a comparable strategy. Her declaration of a state of emergency over birth rates led, under circumstances that smacked of compulsion, to the sterilisation of 8 million Indians, mostly poor and lower-caste people for whom children were some compensation for lives of back-breaking labour. Similar programs were adopted — with similar results — in Mexico, Bolivia, Peru, Indonesia, and Bangladesh.[20] In China, the one-child policy led to millions of forced sterilisations, sex-selective abortions, and even infanticide before its abandonment in 2015.

Though Ehrlich himself publicly decried authoritarianism, it's difficult to see how else his ideas could have been implemented other than through repression, since, by his own argument, the increase in birth rates resisted more gentle measures. The inability of people to stop breeding on their own accord led him, for instance, to advise the US government to withhold aid from any developing nation with an expanding population 'unless that nation convinces us that it is doing everything possible to limit its population'.[21]

In theory, the diagnosis of overpopulation did not discriminate, holding every individual equally guilty merely because they existed. In practice, however, it usually manifested as a hostility from wealthy people in the developed world toward the teeming masses of the poor. In his book, Ehrlich explained how he'd first come to understand the case for population control 'emotionally' during a visit to Delhi, writing of returning with his wife and daughter to their hotel in a decrepit taxi, infested with fleas, when the driver took the barely functioning vehicle into a slum. It was a hot evening, hazy with dust and smoke, but what alarmed Ehrlich most were the crowds:

People eating, people washing, people sleeping. People visiting, arguing, and screaming. People thrusting their hands through the taxi window, begging. People defecating and urinating. People clinging to buses. People herding animals. People, people, people, people.[22]

What makes the passage so revelatory is that, at the time, only 2.8 million people lived in Delhi, a fraction of the 8 million inhabiting Paris. Yet Ehrlich would not have reacted with equal fear and revulsion to, say, crowds on the Avenue des Champs-Élysées.[23] His visceral response — his emotional 'understanding' — did not pertain simply to people so much as those people in particular, with his horror echoing the reaction by Grant and his coterie to the degenerate species that threatened the 'precious things' they cherished. In that taxi, Ehrlich recoiled from the experience of poverty — and then blamed the poor for upsetting him.

Considerable institutional support for the new anti-population theorists came, not surprisingly, from organisations previously associated with Madison Grant-style eugenics: bodies such as the Population Reference Bureau, the Population Council, the Office of Population Research, and the Pioneer Fund. Osborn and Vogt both developed their ideas from within the eugenics movement, as did Garrett Hardin.

That background informed the ideological brutality they espoused. Vogt, for instance, suggested that a high death rate constituted 'one of the greatest national assets' of poor countries, and described fatal diseases as 'blessings in disguise'. Hardin argued (in his 1974 'Lifeboat Ethics: the case against helping the poor'), that rich countries such as the US should not assist the developing world, for that would merely encourage the masses to breed. He also insisted that Americans should reject an immigration policy that might sink the American boat. 'It is unlikely,' Hardin said, 'that civilisation and dignity can survive everywhere but better in a few places than in none. Fortunate minorities must act as the trustees of a civilisation that is threatened by uninformed good intentions.'[24]

Ehrlich himself identified as a liberal. Yet, while immigration did not feature in *The Population Bomb*, he later came to support border exclusion. In the co-authored book *The Golden Door*, he warned against the threat posed by the 67 million Mexicans across the southern border, who were enviously eyeing the privileged lifestyle of Americans. He acknowledged that 'bigots' focussed on what he called the threat of invasion 'by a horde of illegal immigrants', but insisted that 'concerned citizens' were right to wonder why, if they were limiting their own family sizes to preserve the environment, America should 'throw open our doors to over-reproducers'?[25]

On arrival, immigrants embraced American ways, he argued, and that meant they depleted more resources than if they had stayed in their native land with its more frugal customs. By leaving the developing world, they reduced pressure for their homeland to solve its own overpopulation, even as they brought their 'high fertility habits' with them to the US. On that basis, he said, environmentalists should oppose Third World immigration.

The argument, or variations of it, led many prominent environmentalist figures from the 1970s (including David Brower, Dave Foreman, and Earth Day founder Gaylord Nelson) to denounce immigration. For instance, books such as *Desert Solitaire* and *The Monkey Wrench Gang* made Edward Abbey the spiritual leader of so-called Deep Ecology. But Abbey's uncompromising defence of America's wild places also accompanied polemics against what he called 'the mass influx of … millions of hungry, ignorant, unskilled, and culturally morally genetically impoverished people'.[26]

In America today, many of the groups and activists campaigning against migrants can still be linked to a network of conservationists and populationists that emerged in the 1970s.[27] For instance, the claims about illegal aliens used by Donald Trump in his first national campaign advertisements came from the Center for Immigration Studies, one of the many organisations associated with a man called John Tanton.[28] Tanton's career began in the late 1950s as an activist in the Wilderness Society, the Sierra Club, the Audubon Society, the Michigan Natural Areas Council, the Bear Rivers Development Commission, and the Little Traverse Conservancy, among others.

His populationism led him to chair the Sierra Club's National Population Committee and to help establish Zero Population Growth. In the 1970s, he began agitating against immigration, along similar lines to those argued by Ehrlich. In the course of his work, he met with white supremacists, promoted anti-Semitism, and declared the need for America to maintain its 'European-American majority'. He eventually became what *The Washington Post* called the 'mastermind of the modern-day movement to curb immigration', either forming or working with some of the major anti-immigrant bodies of recent times, including the Center for Immigration Studies (CIS), the Federation of American Immigration Reform (FAIR), Californians for Population Stabilization (CAPS), and many others.[29]

Despite the invocation of 'ecofascism' by the white supremacist behind the 2019 Christchurch massacre, most people who describe themselves as environmentalists today loathe and despise Tanton and his ilk. The anti-immigrant tendency within mainstream American environmentalism was decisively defeated during the 1980s and the 1990s by activists intent on linking the defence of the natural world with campaigns for social justice. Such people noted that the obsession with population control made environmentalism unattractive to people of colour, who suspected that their communities would be the first to be sterilised.

As a backlash developed at the brutality justified by populationism in the developing world, environmental organisations shifted their rhetoric to champion female empowerment and poverty amelioration, accepting the argument that immiseration wasn't generated by large families, but rather that large families resulted from immiseration.[30]

The retreat was also driven by the persistent failure of the predicted Malthusian catastrophe to materialise. Birth rates in the developed world had, in fact, already been falling when Ehrlich published his book — and, contrary his prognosis, they continued to fall thereafter. Most experts agree that fertility rates must exceed 2.1 for a population to replace itself — and the average fertility rate across the European Union now sits at about 1.6.[31] Other countries' rates are higher, but the world's population increase continues to slow, so much so that the UN expects total numbers to stabilise by the end of the century.[32] In general, population growth correlates with prosperity, with birth rates slowing as standards of living increase — a relationship that confounds any simple model of out-of-control breeding.

In the modern world, poverty and famine have almost never resulted from absolute shortages. On the contrary, millions starved in the midst of surpluses, prevented from obtaining food by political and economic crises, rather than by nature 'executing her own orders'. Far more people live in New York City than Mogadishu, but that comparison guarantees neither hunger in the Big Apple nor plenty in Somalia. Demographic statistics on their own could not explain why wholesalers allowed unused grain to accumulate instead of feeding the starving, or why corrupt regimes cultivated hunger to maintain social control. Humanity's complex and changing relationship with the Earth could not be reduced to Ehrlich's simple arithmetic. Widespread inequality ensured that population size, in and of itself, revealed very little about resource usage, since a small quantity of the very wealthy typically consumed far more than large numbers of the poor.[33]

The increase in births noted by Ehrlich was real. But, as we have seen, the intensification of environmental depletion in the post-war era stemmed from shifts in industrial production. American corporations were not churning out more commodities to satisfy the growing population, but rather desperately sought to induce more consumption because capital needed to grow.

The falsification of Ehrlich's predictions thus represented something more than slipshod calculations. The science-fictional scenario of people crowding out every centimetre of the galaxy made mathematical sense: obviously, at the most abstract level, only a certain number of bodies can fit within a finite space. In the real world, however, the important limits affecting humans have always been social, shaped less by maths than by the dynamics of particular societies.

In other words, the deep misanthropy that populationism encouraged within environmentalism was never warranted. By its nature, the theory held ordinary people as responsible as their leaders for the problems it diagnosed. Vogt, for instance, explicitly declared everyone equally guilty. 'I mean every person who reads a newspaper printed on pulp from vanished forests,' he said. 'I mean every man and woman who eats a meal drawn from steadily shrinking lands.'[34]

But how did the person who read a newspaper exert the same agency as the media corporation that owned it? What sense does it make to blame men and women for eating (something they can scarcely avoid), rather than focussing on the burger company bulldozing the Amazon to raise its cattle?

Because populationists saw birth rates at fault, they inevitably let the powerful off the hook. The companies, they said, didn't make us breed. Rather, corporate malfeasance resulted from our fecundity, with businesses desperately trying to feed all those hungry new mouths. In 1970, Ehrlich thus explained to *Newsweek* that the 'real villains' in the environmental crisis were not industrialists, but the 'consumers who demand … faster, bigger, cheaper playthings without counting the cost in a dirtier, smellier, sicklier world'.[35]

The neo-Malthusian claim that environmental destruction resulted primarily from overpopulation necessarily absolved social or political structures from blame. It shifted responsibility from the corporations churning out disposable commodities, and blamed instead the people who consumed them. In Ehrlich's numbers game, a mine worker counted the same as the CEO of a coal company, despite the obvious differences in their circumstances.

As a result, the theory gave activists very little in the way of genuine agency. They could choose not to have kids; they could campaign for birth control; and they could, as Ehrlich urged at one stage, write letters to editors to 'complain bitterly about any positive treatment of large families' in the press.[36]

But, at base, they could do little to solve the crisis. For Ehrlich, they *were* the crisis: merely by being alive, they used up the planet. For Ehrlich and his followers, the people were a liability — and that was a message with which both companies and governments could agree.

Populationism thus contributed greatly to a general pessimism about the possibility of environmental action. While the 1970s-style obsession with birth rates has subsided, it has left a significant legacy, one you can still hear echoed every time someone blames the masses for climate change. That's why understanding the bankruptcy of populationism still matters.

People aren't the problem. Rabbits might mindlessly and inevitably breed themselves into extinction. But humans aren't rabbits — and so do not require culling, or sterilising, or extermination by self-appointed park wardens. All the evidence suggests that, in an empowered society, fertility tends to stabilise as women make their own decisions as to when and how they will have children. More importantly, humans can change the way they relate to each other and to the environment. In many countries, a relatively small population consumes vast amounts of resources; in the poorest nations, large numbers live on almost nothing. The numbers themselves matter far less than the social structures upon which they rest.

Environmentalism does not need the Reverend Malthus's hostility to the fecundity of the poor. Other people don't have to be our enemies in a zero-sum struggle for resources. We don't occupy a lifeboat, adrift in dangerous seas. We live in a human community — and we can work together to make it fairer both to people and to the environment on which we all depend.

CHAPTER ELEVEN

War on Nature

In a 2002 essay about environmentalism and politics, the Australian novelist Amanda Lohrey confessed her own youthful enthusiasm for the 1972 hydroelectric project that destroyed Tasmania's exquisite Lake Pedder:

> At the time, I was an active member of Labor Youth and I supported the flooding of the lake, as did most of my political cohort ... The dams were an awe-inspiring marvel, something to be proud of, and the Tasmanian Labor politicians of the day were proud of them, seeing in the dams an emblem of how radical public spending could help lift a community out of the misery of the Depression years and into a better world ... The ALP Premier at the time, Eric Reece, proclaimed the new view on the site of Pedder to be just as 'scenic' as the old ... Dams were not merely dams, they were monuments in a natural landscape; a new and technocratic model of pastoral beauty.[1]

That description evoked the difference between the Old Left and the emerging environmental movement. Old-school socialists often understood people protesting against industrial development as, at best, middle-class dreamers and, at worst, elitists hostile to the needs of working people. For leftists in the second half of the twentieth century, progress meant, almost by definition, a steady increase in human mastery over the world, with the correct use of science and technology enabling us to bend nature, ever more completely, to our desires.

That anti-environmentalism might seem puzzling, given the importance of the natural world to the early labour movement. As we have seen, the exile of ordinary people from their land led to the formation of the working class. In 1770, the Irish writer Oliver Goldsmith documented the catastrophic effects of enclosures in his famous poem 'The Deserted Village':

> No more thy glassy brook reflects the day,
> But choked with sedges, works its weedy way;
> … Ill fares the land, to hastening ills a prey
> Where wealth accumulates, and men decay.
> … But times are altered; trade's unfeeling train
> Usurp the land, and dispossess the swain;
> Along the lawn, where scattered hamlets rose,
> Unwieldy wealth and cumbrous pomp repose.[2]

When the land fares ill, Goldsmith implies, so, too, do people. Along the same lines, Ernest Jones — the poet of the Chartists, one of the first mass labour organisations — depicts the separation from nature as symptomatic of the industrial deprivation he decries, writing of men and women in the new factories longing for 'one fresh touch of dewy grasses' as they endure the 'fume and roar' of the city and its 'heavy, choking air'.[3]

But, precisely because industrialisation heightened the gulf between the cities and the country, working-class life gradually became more and more removed from the natural world. In the

1840s, one Chartist organiser recalled how, in his childhood 'the very trees possessed an individuality', and 'the balmy air was laden with the hum of unseen insects'. In his adulthood, however, he confronted a featureless and grey landscape where 'animal life appeared to be extinct' and no plants grew.

'Nature,' he concluded, 'was out of fashion, and the world seemed to get on tolerably well without her.'[4]

Subsequent generations lived and died on those grimy, cobbled streets. The wealthy and the leisured could admire the countryside, but workers inhabited places from which birds and plants and animals had been for the most part excluded. Labour still reshaped nature (for that is what labour means), but the reshaping took place in urban factories in which organic substances were treated only as raw materials for manufacture.

With the real relationship between work and the world thus obscured, nature could seem — to workers as well as their bosses — as something extraneous, an external resource that could be safely plundered.

In that respect, the attitudes reported by Lohrey expressed the experience of urban life: a common-sense recognition of how capitalism worked. We all know we need jobs. We all know that big engineering projects create them.

But the enthusiasm she documented also reflected specific ideological developments on the left — and, in particular, the overwhelming importance of the Soviet Union, which, for most of the twentieth century, influenced radicals and social democrats alike.

The early years of the Russian Revolution opened tremendous possibilities for conservationism, not least because the expropriation of the autocracy immediately raised questions as to how the country's vast feudal estates might be better managed.

Almost at once, the revolutionary government issued a decree,

'On Land', making trees, water, and minerals the property of the state. A similar decree, 'On Forests', nominated protected zones to secure water basins, stop erosion, and preserve 'monuments of nature', while Lenin signed off on measures regulating the hunting of wild animals such as goats and moose.[5]

Most importantly of all, the Soviet regime established a system of *zapovedniki* (natural reserves) intended to facilitate the study of particular ecologies. Under the auspices of the Commissariat for Enlightenment (that is, education) the *zapovedniki* enabled researchers to analyse intact ecosystems, so as to understand the processes operating in them and then make recommendations about the human interventions that might be appropriate. The pioneer naturalist Vladimir Vladimirovich Stanchinskii used field work in the Ukrainian *zapovedniki* to examine how both herbivores and carnivores used the energy that plants captured from the sun. His understanding of ecological systems allowed him to present a scientific rebuttal to the then widespread enthusiasm for the introduction of exotic plants and animals.[6]

By 1929, more than sixty *zapovedniki* had been created, covering an area of more than 4 million hectares, and fostering, for a brief period, an ecological science significantly in advance of the West.[7]

Unfortunately, by then, the hopes of 1917 had been well and truly dashed, as a growing bureaucratic caste abandoned the dream of worldwide revolution under the pragmatic slogan of 'socialism in one country'. Stalin, the leader of this faction, declared that, rather than transforming the capitalist West, Russia should outcompete it, developing itself into a military and industrial superpower.

'We are fifty to one hundred years behind the most advanced countries,' he declared in 1931. 'We must close this gap in the span of ten years. Either we do that or they will sweep us away.'[8]

Closing the gap meant transforming a backward and largely agricultural nation into an industrialised economy supporting a modern military. The so-called Stalin Revolution that began with the first Five-Year Plan reshaped all of Soviet society, as the USSR threw resources at heavy industry and infrastructure.

From the late 1920s, Russia industrialised at breakneck speed. Figures vary, but, according to some estimates, the first Five-Year plan spurred a 50 per cent increase in industrial output, with a growth rate at an astonishing 18 per cent.[9] Heavy industry, in particular, bounded ahead. Between 1929 and 1934 alone, Soviet industry developed new competencies in making synthetic rubber, motorcycles, wristwatches, cameras, excavators, high-grade cement, and various kinds of steels.[10] The second Five-Year Plan brought significantly less dramatic results, and the outbreak of war interrupted the third. Nevertheless, the eventual Soviet victory over Nazi Germany demonstrated the new industrial might of a country that emerged from the Second World War as a bona fide superpower.

But Stalinist modernisation also meant a distinctive attitude to the natural world — one embodied in the extraordinary slogan 'War on Nature'. As they sought to catch up to the West, the Soviet authorities treated the environment as itself an incarnation of the backwardness they wanted to quell. One regime scientist explained proudly that henceforth 'all living nature will live, thrive and die at none other than the will of man and according to his designs', while an educational guide to the Five-Year Plan duly informed readers that 'the conscious, organised, planned labour of man now fashions rivers and lakes, plants forests and transforms deserts, moderates and accelerates the flow of waters, creates new substance and new species of plants and animals'.[11]

Not unsurprisingly, the long-term environmental effects of Stalin's War on Nature proved utterly disastrous. In 1990, shortly before the communist regime collapsed, the agronomist and dissident Zhores Medvedev noted the dire effects of radiation, artificial flooding, salinisation, dust, salt storms, and a changing water table. On his assessment, the total cultivated land in the Soviet Union had declined by one million hectares a year since 1975.[12]

By the early 1990s, the intensity of air pollution in Soviet industrial centres was such that drivers relied on headlights during daylight merely to navigate safely. The deadly consequences for public health led residents of Nizhny Tagil, a steel town in the Urals, to erect a monument commemorating 'the victims of the ecological terror'.[13]

The sentiment expressed in Nizhny Tagil revealed something fundamental about the Stalinist system: simply, that ecological destruction and political violence proceeded hand-in-hand. Almost by definition, Stalin's new approach to the environment necessitated the repression of environmentalists. As the authorities announced the transformation of the *zapovedniki* into productive units, regime loyalists denounced the scientists working on them as 'saboteurs'. Stanchinskii was arrested, imprisoned, and tortured, eventually dying in custody in 1942.

The persecution of environmentalists paralleled a repression extended into every crevice of society. The Great Purges of 1935 focussed initially on oppositionists, but then spread throughout the party and, eventually, Russia as a whole. Best estimates suggest that, by 1938, nearly three million people were enduring some form of detention, as the gulag system grew and grew and grew.

Many of the regime's most grandiose engineering schemes, such as the White Sea Baltic Canal Project, relied directly on forced labour. *Belomor*, a book that Maxsim Gorky co-ordinated to celebrate the canal's construction, lauds Stalin's leadership as follows:

Stalin holds a pencil. Before him lies a map of the region. Deserted shores. Remote villages. Virgin soil, covered with boulders. Primeval forests. Too much forest as a matter of fact;

it covers the best soil: And swamps. The swamps are always crawling about, making life dull and slovenly. Tillage must be increased. The swamps must be drained …[14]

The canal's construction relied on some 170,000 gulag inmates, working with primitive tools under the direction of armed guards. Some 25,000 prisoners died in the course of its completion.[15] In the battle with nature, they were, quite literally, conscripts.

Yet, for the economy as a whole, the forced-labour camps mattered less for their material contribution and more for their ideological effect.

Stalin might have proclaimed an intent to build 'Socialism in One Country'. But his efforts to outproduce the West led to the adoption of a state-driven system of capital accumulation. His policies replicated, in the space of a few years, the industrialisation that in other countries was associated with the rise of private capitalism. Specifically, the Soviet regime oversaw a massive and incredibly rapid transformation of rural peasants into urban workers — a transformation that, just as elsewhere, rested on the implicit (and sometimes explicit) deployment of violence. During the first Five-Year Plan period alone, repression and hunger meant that more than ten million people moved off the land to become wage earners in major Soviet cities.

The factory owners in early modern England used a combination of ideology (delivered in schools and churches) and punishments (such as restrictive laws and fines) to acclimatise former peasants to wage labour. But there the creation of a working class took place in a piecemeal fashion over the course of the century. In Russia, the state drove the transition at unparalleled speed — and so relied upon an immense infrastructure of coercion.

In October 1930, the regime prohibited the free movement of workers, and then banned factories from rehiring those who had quit a job without permission. Eventually, tsarist internal passports — a hated system, immediately abolished after the revolution — were restored. By 1932, a single day's absence for work became grounds for instant dismissal, with employees personally responsible for any inadvertent damage to raw material or equipment. The authorities cut unemployment relief and introduced criminal sanctions — including, eventually, the death penalty — for violating factory discipline.

The gulags represented the most extreme form of this general phenomenon.

'The White Sea Baltic Canal,' enthused *Pravda* in 1933, 'will go down in history as more than a school of the newest technology of hydroconstruction. It will also go down in history as a school of massive re-education, of the re-making of people led astray from the path of labour.'[16]

The book *Belomor* illustrates what this 're-making' meant. With the completion of the canal, Maxim Gorky celebrates 'the victory over nature accomplished' by the prisoners and the 'more amazing' victory they 'have gained over themselves'.[17]

Like early modern Britain, an industrialising Soviet Russia needed to acclimatise millions of men and women to ways of working, ways of living, and ways of relating to nature that were quite foreign to them. As in Britain, the new system required a new kind of person: someone who had internalised the discipline of wage labour. The term used in the camps was *perekovka* — literally, 'reforging'.

Gorky, and other regime apologists, presented *perekovka* as an example of Marx's notion that people change themselves as they change the world. It represented precisely the opposite. Marx wrote of men and women taking control of the labour that makes them human and, as a result, becoming more completely who they were. In Stalin's Russia, *perekovka* signified the submission of labourers to external discipline. The reforged inmates abandoned their own will;

they learned to destroy nature as directed by supervisors.

As in Britain, explicit repression was accompanied by ideological persuasion. That's why Stalin summoned Gorky and his *Belomor* co-writers to a special meeting.

'Man is remade by life itself,' the dictator told them. 'But you, too, will assist in remaking his soul. This is important, the production of human souls. That's why I raise my glass to writers, to the engineers of the human soul.'[18]

To shape souls, authors lauded the regime and its leaders, and promoted an increasingly conservative ideal of citizenship. After 1917, the Bolsheviks introduced no-fault divorce, legalised homosexuality, promoted contraception and access to abortion, and encouraged women to engage in public life. The Stalin revolution saw an idealisation of traditional motherhood (with women who bore more than seven children receiving awards), abortion banned, divorce made more difficult, and homosexuality recriminalised. The approved novels celebrated, in other words, precisely the kind of values that the English capitalists tried to promote among their workers.

But they also denounced the natural world. Throughout the literature of the time, the war on nature provided a common metaphor for the regime's struggle with Trotskyites, kulaks, or other internal saboteurs, in an art intended to acclimatise a newly formed working class to modern industrial production.[19]

Gorky himself campaigned specifically against traditional nature poetry. He urged writers to eschew 'feelings of submissiveness [or] adulation' towards mountains, landscapes, or the wild. 'Praise of nature is praise of a despot,' he insisted. Socialist writers could not remain silent about the natural calamities that 'destroy thousands of lives and ruin the fruits of the people's labour'. Rather than celebrating nature, they should, he said, summon the working class to fight against its 'foul tricks'.[20]

The 'success' of Stalin's industrialisation made the Soviet experience a tremendously influential model of development.

In China, for instance, Mao sought to compete with Britain and other imperial nations through a program modelled very closely on Stalinist Russia and reliant on Soviet specialists. As in Russia, the transformation of labour mandated a massive propaganda campaign directed at a peasant population. Under the slogan 'Man Must Conquer Nature', Mao launched gargantuan engineering projects, and urged the population to cut down forests, telling them that 'Man's ability to know and change nature is unlimited.' As in Russia, the war on nature entailed horrific repression: camps, summary imprisonment, executions, widespread torture, and so on.

Not surprisingly, this approach subjected China to all manner of environmental disasters: toxic air in the cities, the pollution of mainland rivers and lakes, and the salinisation, erosion, deforestation, overgrazing, and persistent flooding of the land.[21]

Nevertheless, versions of state-driven industrialisation were embraced across Eastern Europe, in Nehru's India, and many other nations, usually with the same destructive outcomes.[22]

In the West, an idea of nature as something that humans could or should reshape at will became widespread on the left. Most of those who lauded the 'drive to modernisation' that Lohrey discussed were not enthusiasts for Stalinist terror. Rather, they sought to deliver employment and services for working-class people, and they understood the conquest of nature as a means to that end.

Nevertheless, the hydroelectric project constructed on Lake Pedder flooded a unique ecosystem, washing away the area's distinctive beauty. The dam led to the extinction of at least three species unknown anywhere else: the Lake Pedder planarian (a kind of carnivorous worm), the Lade Pedder earthworm, and a small fish known as the Pedder galaxias.[23]

That might not have seemed much of a sacrifice — a couple

of worms and a fish — in the face of the perceived benefits. But those creatures are now gone forever, an existential depletion that no scientist or engineer can ever restore.

Furthermore, the intensifying accretion of similar losses, all across the planet, makes increasingly obvious the centrality of nature to all humanity, especially working-class people. The pragmatic valorisation of 'jobs' (whatever those jobs might entail) and the technocratic focus on infrastructure fails to consider the more fundamental question: namely, why should the basic requirements of life require the destruction of the natural world to which humanity belongs? No matter the banner under which the war on the environment takes place, the perception of nature as entirely distinct and separate from human society reflects a historical disempowerment of the population, an original act of violence perpetrated on working people.

CHAPTER TWELVE

Social Murder

'I've got a constant asthma cough and I'm constantly breathless, and my throat is really impacted as well.' That was how high school teacher Gabrielle Wenman described living in Sydney in early 2020.[1]

Back then, much of the country was burning. The journal *Nature* later called the 2019–20 Australian bushfire season 'unprecedented', noting the number of different fires, the extraordinary range of the territory ablaze, and the ferocity of the heat.[2]

But a lack of precedent didn't make the disaster unexpected.

As far back as 2003, researchers had concluded that 'climate change throughout the present century is predicted to lead to increased temperatures and, with them, a heightened risk of unplanned fire'.[3] The next year, the National Inquiry on Bushfire Mitigation and Management put the same argument to the Council of Australian Governments, and a few years later, in 2008, scientists explained that the risk would become readily apparent by 2020 — which is, more or less, precisely what transpired.

The fires began in September 2019, and worsened through the following months. On 31 December, the year ended with tourists at the seaside resort of Mallacoota sheltering in the ocean, awaiting rescue by the navy as encroaching fires turned the sky around them a lurid and terrifying orange. The blazes continued into 2020, burning some 186,000 square kilometres, destroying nearly 6,000 buildings, and killing thirty-four people. Perhaps 3 billion animals either died or were displaced.[4]

For weeks, smoke blanketed some of Australia's largest cities, blocking the sun with an acrid cloud of ash, embers, and particles. The pollution level in in Sydney reached twelve times the measure usually deemed hazardous. On occasions, visibility was reduced to just 500 metres, and the government urged people to stay inside with their windows and doors closed.

The disaster did not affect the population equally. How could it? As one academic study of the Australian fires explained:

> Although authorities ... advised avoiding bushfire smoke by staying indoors and by using air conditioning when possible, or in severe cases air purifiers, there are socio-economic factors which make it challenging for financially vulnerable groups to implement these measures and housing standards.[5]

Notoriously, Prime Minister Scott Morrison flew to Hawaii during the worst of the crisis. Most people, though, had no choice but to see it through, which often meant working in jobs that exposed them to toxic particles. In those weeks, sore throats, inflamed eyes, and persistent coughs became common. A subsequent study suggested that smoke put more than 4,000 people in hospital, and led to the deaths of 445.[6]

James Maitland once listed 'air' as the paradigm of public wealth, something both needed by everyone and accessible to them. In Australia, however, clean, sweet, and breathable air became a privilege, guaranteed only to the few.

In his 1845 *Condition of the Working Class in England in 1844*, Engels describes as 'social murder' the pollution in cities such as

Manchester, places in which 'the lungs of the inhabitants fail to receive the due supply of oxygen'. The men and women of his day could, like Wenman, scarcely breathe: capitalism meant, he wrote bitterly, that they lived 'under conditions in which they [could] neither retain health nor life'.[7]

Yet the efforts of Manchester labourers to improve their housing and their workplaces weren't necessarily recognised as battles to preserve nature. They lived next to stagnant canals, alongside redbrick factories and cobbled streets. What did 'nature' mean to them? It was the wealthy and the privileged who could admire 'wildernesses', places precious because of their difference from the dead zones that capital had created.

In 2020, by contrast, no one in Australia thought the bushfire smoke a product of the cities. The taste of ash in the back of your throat and the charred eucalyptus at your feet: these things were manifestly consequences of humanity's dysfunctional interaction with the natural world.

It's not a distinctly Australian experience, either. Global heating makes fires worse everywhere. A recent *Guardian* study demonstrated that places in California, Siberia, and Pantanal that never used to burn now catch fire with increasing regularity.[8]

The disasters unleashed by climate change increasingly reverse the older polarities. If, in the past, wealth afforded you the leisure to worry about nature, today it gives you the option of indifference, with your status insulating you from the environmental crises experienced by the less fortunate as an immediate — sometimes even existential — peril.

Already, heat kills more Australians than floods, cyclones, bushfires, or other natural disasters do. In New South Wales, the more-expensive suburbs (such as the harbour and coastal areas) are generally the coolest, while the working-class areas of Western Sydney are notoriously hot, with Penrith recording a temperature of

48.9c during the 2020 fires. As the world warms, experts say, parts of the west (the places inhabited by the poorest) will probably have to be abandoned.[9]

A crisis of Biblical scale, we might say: one in which, as the Book of Matthew tells us, the little that the poor man has shall be taken away.

The inequity inherent in our twenty-first–century environmental disaster creates opportunities for a new and different kind of environmentalism. To date, the connection between global warming and capitalism has often remained blandly abstract, an intellectual association quite distant from the everyday experiences of ordinary people. Understandably, campaigners sometime presented the big picture (such as global heating, and mournful polar bears on ice-floes), and moved from that to actions that individuals might take (such as recycling, voting a certain way, or attending a march) in their own lives.

But the growing severity of ecological breakdown provides a chance to reverse that sequence, with an environmentalism firmly embedded in class relations.

In 1971, the Australian construction firm AV Jennings announced it would build new luxury houses in the well-to-do Sydney suburb of Hunters Hill — a plan that meant bulldozing Kelly's Bush, a major tract of remnant forest on the western part of the lower Parramatta River.[10]

No one at the company expected problems. The clear-felling of Australian bush had been a national preoccupation for nearly 200 years, and, with Sydney in the grip of one of its regular development frenzies, scrub was being bulldozed with a renewed enthusiasm. The only objections to the Hunters Hill plan came from a group of middle-class women — and they had been consistently rebuffed by all the politicians they had approached for help.

But then the women did something unexpected. They called the

New South Wales Builders Labourers Federation (BLF).

In the 1970s, genteel ladies from the lower North Shore did not, as a rule, converse with rough and unlettered militants from building sites, especially since the BLF was already known for its radicalism. Its leading activists — Jack Mundey, Bob Pringle, and Joe Owens — had emerged from a rank-and-file group devoted to democratising the union and clearing out the criminality of the industry. They'd established regular membership meetings, promised to rotate leadership roles, and linked the remuneration of officials to that of the men. They also talked, loudly and publicly, about the need for unions to support the social activism of the times.

The Hunters Hill women had heard one such interview. They contacted the union for help. A BLF militant later recalled, 'Those women more or less said, well, here's a chance to put your theory into practice.'[11]

At first, the union leaders hesitated. No one else seemed to care about Kelly's Bush. Why should they? They suggested the women hold a public meeting to judge community sentiment. Hundreds of people attended, in a palpable demonstration of local concern. Duly persuaded, the BLF placed a black ban on constructing the houses, one that held firm even when AV Jennings resorted to non-union labour.

That intervention opened the floodgates. All across Sydney, people fighting against the rampant and destructive development despoiling the city approached the BLF for assistance. Between 1971 and 1974, the BLF stopped — through what became known as 'Green Bans' — some forty-two different projects, said to be worth a total of more than $46 billion.

Some of the Green Bans saved places of natural beauty, locations already cherished by locals for their ambience. In March 1972, architects and environmentalists won support for a ban on a carpark attached the Sydney Opera House, a scheme that would have defaced the land and ancient trees of the nearby Botanical Gardens. The next year, a ban halted the dumping of waste material into green space at Dunbar Park. In October 1973, the BLF ended the destruction of vegetation and ecology on Rileys Island.

But many — perhaps most — of the bans centred on what might be called the urban environment, areas that weren't necessarily thought of as beauty spots, but possessed a particular significance for locals. The BLF placed, for instance, a Green Ban on the construction of the North-Western Expressway that would have dissected the then working-class suburbs of Ultimo, Glebe, Annandale, Rozelle, and Leichhardt. The union led the campaign to save The Rocks, the historic area on the harbour where the poorer settlers had built their higgledy-piggledy dwellings emulating the slums they'd left behind in England. It stopped $400 million of commercial buildings slated for Woolloomooloo; it prevented the much-loved Centennial Park becoming a sports complex.[12]

The Green Ban movement lasted only a few years. By 1975, the more conservative federal branch of the union had intervened in New South Wales and succeeded, to the unabashed joy of employers and the state government, in expelling Mundey and his allies. The corrupt president, Norm Gallagher, shut the New South Wales branch and lifted the remaining bans, sneering as he did so at environmental campaigners as 'residents, sheilas, and poofters' who 'deprived our members of their jobs'.[13]

In the context of the almost existential crisis we face today, a brief campaign initiated by a now-defunct trade union centred in one Australian state nearly half a century ago scarcely seems important. Yet there's a lot still to be learned from the Green Bans.

Some leftists refer to 'classism' to decry the treatment of working people. The term relies on an implicit analogy with racism and sexism to highlight discrimination based on socio-economic status — as, say, when police harass teenagers in a poor neighbourhood in a way they wouldn't in a wealthier one. Certainly, class can, and does, correlate with all kinds of misery and mistreatment. But to understand it merely as an axis of oppression — as 'classism' implies — misses something fundamental.

The concept of class doesn't simply offer a way to talk about injustice. It also provides a basis on which a response to that injustice might be organised, as the Green Bans showed.

The BLF used the union structures to distribute information and propaganda. It mobilised its members to take part in street marches in support of the bans. In some suburbs, its campaigns culminated in residents and unionists physically resisting police and developers, with mass arrests ensuing.

But the Green Bans' significance did not come from any of this. The bans mattered because of the union's industrial power, its willingness and ability to close down production. The original Hunters Hill dispute ended, for instance, when construction workers in North Sydney who were completing an office project for AV Jennings conveyed to the developer a simple message: 'If you attempt to build on Kelly's Bush, even if there is the loss of one tree, this half-completed building will remain so forever, as a monument to Kelly's Bush.'[14]

A contrast with the contemporary School Strike for Climate movement illustrates the weight of that threat. Greta Thunberg initiated a worldwide movement after skipping school, initially by herself, to stand each Friday outside the Swedish parliament holding a home-made sign. Her slogan 'Fridaysforfuture' spread throughout in Sweden, then across Europe and finally internationally. By December 2018, students were walking out of schools in something like 270 cities.

Over the next years, the movement broadened and deepened, moving from schools to the population as a whole. In November 2019, over two million people joined the Fourth Global Climate

Strike: one of the most impressive climate actions yet, with protests in 2,400 cities across 157 different nations.

The student walk-out disrupted their schools and embarrassed the authorities. In Australia, for instance, Prime Minister Scott Morrison responded with an angry declaration that students needed 'more learning ... and less activism'.[15] Marching protesters brought traffic to a halt, and created a dramatic spectacle irresistible to the media.

These mobilisations borrowed their lexicon from the labour tradition. When students walked out of classes to attend climate rallies, they described themselves as 'on strike'. In several countries, trade unions endorsed and joined the events.

The climate strike thus provided a hint of what a global mobilisation centred on organised labour might achieve. Such an event would not simply entail big marches (though they'd surely be part of it). It would also mean workers withdrawing their labour and thus paralysing industry in ways that governments could not ignore. Unlike a protest rally, a strike does more than simply demonstrate sentiment — a strike reveals power.

That's something that's been known ever since 1157 BC, when workers painting the elaborate ritual decorations on a pharaonic tomb on the west bank of Thebes complained about not receiving their rations. In an ancient papyrus, a scribe named Amennakht recorded how the men declared, 'We are hungry!' and then sat down in a temple complex — essentially, launching a strike. When the foremen pleaded with them to get back to work, the men 'swore great oaths' and stayed put. The pharaoh might have been a living god, but he recognised he couldn't build a tomb by himself. He needed workers — and so the strikers duly received their supplies.[16]

Every society, from ancient Egypt to modern America, depends on labour. Even in a digital economy, where algorithms trigger robots to pack goods for delivery, the organised withdrawal of work cannot be ignored. Those who profit from the destruction of nature don't and can't do the destroying themselves. Without workers, the system freezes — and that gives labour tremendous potential power.

Furthermore, because wage labour organises production, it ties people to the structures necessary for capitalism to function. The expansion of capital cannot happen without men and women talking and planning and working together. Businesses — particularly big businesses — depend on the collective labour of everyone they employ. Workers must co-operate within an individual company; they also must co-operate externally, liaising with a chain of customers and suppliers that stretches out across the planet.

This co-operation is almost obligatory, driven by the necessity to expand value. You don't choose your workmates: you either get along with them or else you lose your job. Yet the relationships thus forged can be repurposed. Work brings us into contact with other people — and together with those people, we can organise.

The links that make the system function can, under certain circumstances, bring it to a halt. That's the basis for the old socialist slogan, 'Workers of the world unite': as the writer Marshall Berman put it, the modern working class constitutes 'an immense worldwide community waiting to happen'.[17] If we use the broadest definition of working class — all those who sell their labour power for a wage, as well as their families and dependents — we're describing a huge proportion of the population. This comprises not just building workers, but Uber drivers and IT employees and aged-care staff and teachers, and all manner of other people, of every gender and ethnicity and religion. That's Berman's point. Strikes depend on a unity fostered by the conditions under which we all labour — a unity that, at least potentially, can bring together men and women with nothing else in common other than their class position.

The 1970s were, of course, a long time ago, in a wrenchingly different political period. Today, a mere 10.3 per cent of the workforce in the United States belongs to a union, the lowest figure recorded since the Bureau of Labor Statistics began recording membership in the early 1980s.[18] In Australia, the figures are similar. The most recent statistics record only 14.3 per cent of workers as members, a massive drop from the 1980s, when almost half the workforce carried a union card. The number of days lost to strikes — a good proxy for union power and militancy — stands at an all-time low.

The historical correlation between the decline of organised labour and the intensifying environmental crisis is not accidental. Naomi Klein writes about how climate researchers established the basic science of global warming in the late 1980s, during the so-called neoliberal turn. The political consensus of that era valorised free markets — and excoriated the unionism that impeded them. As a result, 'corporate power was ascendant at the very moment when we needed to exert unprecedented controls over corporate behaviour in order to protect life on Earth'.[19]

Yet we might also wonder if that ascendancy has now created precisely the conditions in which a revived unionism might emerge.

Consider an interesting historical precedent. In Britain, the 1880s saw a social polarisation similar to our own, with the fortunate accumulating wealth on a scale that most ordinary people could scarcely imagine. Then, as now, the great majority of workers did not belong to trade unions. Many progressives feared that core industries would always be unorganisable. On the waterfront, for instance, 90 per cent of workers were casuals, with employers choosing each day's labour from a mob of desperate and unskilled men clamouring for any work they could get. What could solidarity mean to such beaten-down people?

The so-called New Unionism emerged from the efforts of workers at the Bryant and May match company. A factory employing match girls sounds like a cliché of Victorian deprivation, and so it's important to realise that, at the time, Bryant and May was a household name — a brand everyone knew, making products that everyone used. Its owner, Wilberforce Bryant, wasn't considered an ogre. On the contrary, as an urbane and powerful businessman, he consorted socially with the leading politicians of the day.

His factory employed some 1,400 workers — most of them girls under fifteen, and most of them hired as casuals. They weren't union members, and few people believed they ever would be. They were young, they were female, and they laboured under extraordinary discipline, fined by their male foremen if they made mistakes or talked or appeared dirty.

In 1888, the radical journalist Annie Besant published an exposé of the harsh treatment the women endured. In response, management insisted the workers sign a statement distancing themselves from her claims. When three women refused, they were sacked — and most of the factory walked out with them. As one of the workers later recalled, '[It] just went like tinder, one girl began, and the rest said, "Yes", so out we all went.'[20]

The match women organised their own strike committee, and sought backing from other workers and other industries. Within three weeks, Bryant and May, reeling from the speed at which the dispute escalated, capitulated, and the women, who had since formed their own union, were reinstated with improved conditions. A newspaper of the day noted: 'The victory of the girls ... is complete. It was won without preparation — without organisation — without funds.'[21]

The example proved contagious. The following year, gas workers rallied for the eight-hour day, signing up thousands of new members as they did so. In summer 1889, the new mood spread to dock workers, who went out over demands for higher pay. By September, the *East London News* reported that:

[T]he present week might not inaptly be called the week of strikes — coal men; match girls; parcels postmen; car men; rag, bone, and paper porters and pickers. The employees in jam, biscuit, rope, iron, screw, clothing, and railway works have found some grievance, real and imaginary, and have followed the infectious example of coming out on strike.[22]

Crucially, most of the workers had not previously been unionised. Many were impoverished immigrants, from Ireland, in particular. As the *Daily News* argued, 'They were supposed to be struggling so hard for a bare subsistence that they would rather crowd each other out than help each other.'[23] Yet it was from these ragged, desperate people that modern British unionism emerged, as the number of members swelled from a paltry 750,000 in 1888 to more than two million by 1900.

A walkout by match girls in Victorian England might seem irrelevant, almost quaint. Yet, paradoxically, the decline of the union movement means that some of the most modern workplaces resemble facilities from the nineteenth century much more than they do factories from the twentieth.

In her recent book *On the Clock*, Emily Guendelsberger describes taking a job in an Amazon warehouse near Louisville. Amazon, of course, depends on the most cutting-edge technology. But the company supplements the wizardry of its algorithms with management techniques the principles of which would be entirely familiar to Wilberforce Bryant. As labour scholars Jake Alimahomed-Wilson and Ellen Reese explain, 'Amazon's warehouses in many respects resemble the factories of the past: workers are subject to the daily indignities, productivity pressures, and health and safety hazards long associated with manufacturing.'[24]

Guendelsberger learns that her scanner gun tracks everything she does — and she's forced to carry it everywhere, even to the bathroom. Casuals employed as warehouse pickers must move some 360 items an hour, one every 6.7 seconds.[25] Like the women in the match factory, Amazon workers are terminated if they don't meet those productivity targets — if they don't, in Amazon speak, 'make rate'.

Guendelsberger's attempts to make rate at Amazon blur into a month of misery, a haze of 'constant pain, waking up at 4:00 a.m., walking between thirteen and sixteen miles per day, being too tired to talk to anyone, eating a lot of McDonald's, rarely seeing the sun, and passing out the minute I get home from work'.[26]

Besant's exposé of Bryant and May emphasised the toxicity of the industrial process, with the women regularly contracting 'phossy jaw' (white phosphorous poisoning). The hideous condition began with a toothache and flu symptoms before putrid abscesses developed in the workers' gums and cheeks. It caused gross disfigurements, with many sufferers eventually dying from convulsions and haemorrhages in an especially awful form of social murder.

Not every worker contracted full-blown phossy jaw, but all were exposed to pollution and poison. Contemporaries described how the lanes near the factory were regularly marked by the fluorescent vomit of ill women staggering to and from their homes.

Few people in the wealthy world endure comparable hazards today (although the story's different in developing nations). Nevertheless, twenty-first-century employment distinguishes itself by its insecurity, an insecurity linked to genuine health and safety risks. Put simply, many of us feel our jobs to be dangling by a thread, and that precarity means we're more liable to accept dangerous conditions.

For instance, during her time at Amazon, Guendelsberger learns that the warehouse in which she works features an array of vending machines dispensing Tylenol and Advil. She soon understands why:

When my alarm goes off for my second full day of picking, it is the worst my body's felt in my entire life ... *Everything* hurts. My feet are the worst, but my back, shoulders, arms, and neck feel terrible, too. My hips, knees, and thighs ache from all the squats to pick from floor-level drawers. My right wrist, hand, and fingers ache from operating the scanner gun. My right elbow aches from pulling open hundreds of drawers. I even have a throbbing headache.[27]

Hence the painkillers, the company's response to its aching, damaged workforce. A recent leaked internal report from Amazon revealed that its 'fulfillment centers' recorded 14,000 serious injuries in the US in 2019, a rate twice the industry standard. The figure showed a significant rise from only a few years before — a testament, many observers say, to the inhuman pace set by the company's robots. The report itself contained a common explanation from employees as to why they got hurt: '[Work] requires me to move too quickly, so I am forced to either cut corners or not make rate.'[28] The same pressure means that the drivers of Amazon vans ('sweatshops on wheels', as Alimahomed-Wilson and Reese call them) regularly defecate and urinate into bags and pots, unable to pause for the most intimate human necessities.[29]

Workers with more secure employment might have felt confident enough to complain. 'You don't really believe the peeing in bottles thing, do you?' scoffed the Amazon Twitter account. 'If that were true, nobody would work for us.' (The company later recanted this retort). But behind the indignities and the injuries looms an American economy in which many of Guendelsberger's workmates proclaim themselves fortunate to be picking at Amazon, because their other options are so markedly worse. Most low-wage employers use digital technology to time every second of labour; most employ algorithmic scheduling to ensure they allocate the least possible quantity of staff at any time.

Guendelsberger writes of expecting to find Amazon's system uniquely strict. In fact, she discovers that most jobs available to unskilled workers use the same kind of productivity-managing techniques. She concludes:

It's *normal* to have your thirty-minute lunch timed down to the second. It's *normal* to work through pain and illness. It's *normal* to have *time to lean, time to clean* enforced by constant monitoring and beeping.[30]

The biggest private employer in the United States (even without counting its army of 'independent' subcontractors), Amazon establishes practices emulated everywhere. It is now America's second-biggest clothing seller, as well as the largest retailer of books, toys, shoes, and many other consumer items. It's the fifth-largest grocery business, and the fastest-growing logistics provider.[31] In all those fields, its competitors must adopt Amazon-style methods to keep up. As the company spreads across Europe and the global south, it normalises the industrial techniques associated with what some have dubbed 'surveillance capitalism' (even as it sells the methods developed for monitoring its workers to police forces and state agencies).[32]

In the 1880s, phossy jaw was experienced as a purely industrial issue. Today, by contrast, the worsening environmental crisis increasingly exposes the relationship between industry and nature, simply because climate change increases the danger in dangerous jobs. If environmental crises disproportionately affect working-class people, they affect us most of all when we are at work, the place where we spend most of our days, under conditions not of our choosing.

Australian scholars Freya Newman and Elizabeth Humphrys recently discussed the growing impact of climactic heat stress on construction workers, particularly those precariously employed. Global heating has made work more dangerous — and this, they suggest, is a general phenomenon.[33]

At Amazon, for instance, warehouse staff speak of an 'Amazon pace', a rate midway between running and walking necessary to meet their required quotas. They describe the constant exertion as equivalent to jogging on a treadmill.

'They constantly were on our case to go faster, in everything we did,' said one worker. 'So I would be sorting, either in the aisles or on the conveyer belt, and I would have sweat just dripping down from me because I was working so hard and there wasn't any air conditioning.'[34]

The necessity for that exertion means that, on hot days, heatstroke often overcomes workers in the stifling warehouses — and, of course, climate change is making hot days more and more common.

During the Covid pandemic, Amazon CEO Jeff Bezos grew his wealth by about $70 billion, as a locked-down public's reliance on online shopping made him one of the wealthiest people in human history. (According to one estimate, he earned the annual salary of his lowest-paid employee every eleven seconds.)[35]

But that increased demand brought more and more casual staff into the Amazon warehouses, forcing its workers into dangerous proximity with each other. Desperate to meet the spike in orders, management jammed more people in, rather than allowing proper distancing. Staff complained that, in the canteen, they were pressed shoulder-to-shoulder. Masks weren't mandatory, and staff had to specially request disinfectant gel.

By October 2020, some 20,000 Amazon employees were infected with Covid.[36]

It would be wrong to describe the pandemic as a straightforward and direct consequence of global warming. But it would be equally mistaken to deny any connection. By definition, zoonotic diseases — viruses that jump from animals to people — hinge on the human relationship with nature. Factory farming, deforestation, the commodification of exotic creatures, uncontrolled urbanisation: all these factors exacerbate the risk of new pandemics.[37]

'You look at climate change, we have transformed the nature of the Earth,' explained Aaron Bernstein from Harvard's Center for Climate, Health, and the Global Environment:

> We have fundamentally changed the composition of the atmosphere, and as such, we shouldn't be surprised that that affects our health. We have, as a species, grown up in partnership with the planet and life we live with. So, when we change the rules of the game, we shouldn't expect that it wouldn't affect our health, for better or worse. That's true of the climate. And the same principle holds for the emergence of infections.[38]

The twenty-first-century capitalism that helped Covid emerge also created the particular conditions that allowed it to spread. As UN secretary António Guterres said, the consequences of the pandemic fell 'disproportionately on the most vulnerable: people living in poverty, the working poor, women and children, persons with disabilities, and other marginalised groups'.[39]

The same might be said of every fresh peril associated with the environmental emergency. From floods to hurricanes, the greatest impact will be felt by working people, and the distinctive social conditions of the twenty-first century will make that impact worse.

'Climate change constantly shapes the experience of work,' Newman and Humphrys write. 'All labour is made insecure by climate change, given it threatens human and ecological life; impacts the capacity of capitalism to maintain stable accumulation; and often negatively impacts the capacity to labour.'[40]

Global warming can't, of course, be reduced to a workplace issue. The transformation of the Earth's natural processes will have consequences for every aspect of our lives. Nevertheless, struggles to unionise precarious work will come under pressure to address climate change, simply because the effects of climate change will be felt by such workers more and more directly.

The company formed by Jeff Bezos shares its name with the broadleaf tropical rainforest extending across north-western Brazil and into Bolivia, Peru, Ecuador, Columbia, Venezuela, Guyana, Suriname, and French Guiana. That Amazon — a place of profound ecological significance — shrinks each year.

The other Amazon continues to expand, spending heavily in Mexico and India and other new markets. The conditions in its warehouses are not legacies of the past. They're anticipations of a rapidly arriving future, one in which employment in both the developed and industrialising world is increasingly regimented, surveilled, and dangerous. The old lie that promised good jobs in return for environmental degradation has become increasingly threadbare, since the most modern work simultaneously ruins work, people, and nature.

None of this makes BLF-style Green Bans campaigns imminent or automatic. In 2021, Amazon successfully defeated a major organising drive among warehouse workers in Bessemer, Alabama, and in doing so showed that there's a long, long way to go to restore union power in the United States,

Still, we should not forget that the Covid epidemic also coincided with the largest, most sustained protest campaign of all in American history, with the polling firm Kaiser Family Foundation suggesting that, in 2020, perhaps 26 million people attended demonstrations of some sort.[41] On 6 June, *The New York Times* identified over 4,700 different rallies since May — an average of 140 per day, with more than 40 per cent of counties throughout America staging some kind of protest.

'I can't breathe,' gasped George Floyd, as a white officer named Derek Chauvin knelt on his neck for more than eight minutes.[42]

His words — another desperate plea for air — became a rallying call for Black Lives Matter, capturing a community's sense of being choked by brutal policing.

The BLM demonstrations were against racism, not the environmental crisis. Yet the scale of the protests — substantially bigger than the iconic anti-war rallies of the Vietnam era — gives the lie to any suggestion of an apathetic and compliant population.

We might, perhaps, differentiate the outrage over Floyd's inability to breathe from the experience of those affected by bushfires or Covid-19 by noting the importance of direct human agency in the murder in Minneapolis. When police choke a man to death, the immediacy of the killing presents an obvious focus for anger.

But, in some ways, that misses the point. For decades, the deaths of black men had been portrayed by the media, the government, and the police themselves as unexceptional, a regrettable but necessary consequence of maintaining an orderly society. As Michelle Alexander argued in her ground-breaking book *The New Jim Crow*, American law enforcement reflected a racialised caste system that 'was largely invisible, even to people, like me, who spent most of their waking hours fighting for justice'.[43] In the city of Ferguson, Missouri (a city of 21,000), an investigation after police shot Michael Brown in 2014 found arrest warrants outstanding for 32,975 offences — a staggering 1.5 offences for every city resident.[44] The absurdity of a town with more crimes than people went unnoticed, precisely because over-policing had been so normalised.

The anger in 2020 reflected an ideological shift, a defamiliarisation of racist policing that allowed activists both to decry individual deaths as murders rather than accidents, and then to link those killings to a systemic problem — one that would only be solved by structural changes such as the abolition of the police.

It was on this basis that demonstrations over Floyd's killing spread all over the world.

That's another reason why, in the fight against climate change, labour matters: industrial organising tends to perform a similar defamiliarisation.

When Jack Mundey died in 2020, *The Sydney Morning Herald* published a laudatory obituary, noting, quite correctly, that without his intervention Sydney's most cherished landscapes and significant sites would have been forever obliterated.[45]

In 1972, however, *The Sydney Morning Herald* had expressed a very different view about Mundey's activities. At the time the Builders Laborers were actually saving Sydney's skyline, the paper polemicised incessantly against him, publishing, within the space of a single twelve-day period, no fewer than five editorials attacking the Green Bans.

'[T]here is something highly comical,' it sniffed, 'in the spectacle of builders labourers, whose ideas on industrial relations do not rise above strikes, violence, intimidation and the destruction of property, setting themselves up as arbiters of taste and protectors of our national heritage.[46]

The sneer in that passage revealed more than old-fashioned snobbery. It expressed a fundamental condition of wage labour. The purchase of any commodity allows the new owner to determine its use. The wage system means employers buy the commodity known as 'labour power' — and, as its owners, feel a right to control it. In that sense, by mocking labourers' pretensions to decide what they did, *The Sydney Morning Herald* neatly articulated the system's logic: workers possessed no rights over the labour they had sold to others.

Yet, when it comes to work, commodity exchange contains a paradox: namely, workers remain stubbornly human, even when treated as objects. *The Sydney Morning Herald*'s editorialist might have expected robotic compliance from labourers; but, with the Green Bans, building unionists showed they could still think and feel and act. By determining, in accordance with the community and their own consciences, what they performed and how, they regained something of their humanity.

Despite the scorn of respectable Sydney, Mundey noted how the workers 'saw the success of the union and felt that the union was contributing something of a social nature, and there was an uplifting in the confidence of the union members'. They began to think of 'social responsibility of workers' and their obligation to examine the 'end result of their labour', which was 'tied right up with the ecological crisis which exists in our society'.[47]

Since time immemorial, ordinary people had put elements of themselves into the labour by which they related to the world. They had, in fact, been 'arbiters of taste' and 'protectors of natural heritage', simply because they made choices about what they would and wouldn't do. Capitalism stripped that away — and the Green Bans restored something of what had been lost.

By imposing the bans, Mundey said, the BLF insisted 'all work performed should be of a socially useful and of an ecologically benign nature'.[48] That necessarily raised questions as to why, most of the time, work wasn't either socially useful or ecologically benign.

To put it another way, the union's efforts drew attention to how people related to each other, how people related to nature, and how the two were connected.

The philosopher Elizabeth Anderson invites us to consider a hypothetical political regime that replaces the rule of law with arbitrary and changeable directives delivered by unaccountable, unelected superiors who must be obeyed without question. In this scenario, most people have no autonomy, and can be instructed on the most personal issues (such as how to dress and wear their hair). Surveillance is ubiquitous; the government can dictate how you speak, make you undergo medical testing, and search your person and possessions.[49]

That regime exists, of course, in every workplace, where what Anderson dubs a 'private government' exerts an authority that we would never accept anywhere else. Most of its time, the legitimacy of that government goes without question, accepted as entirely normal and unexceptional. Emily Guendelsberger, for instance, learns that her co-workers, who live achingly hard lives on the minimum wage, have internalised the algorithmically determined priorities of their bosses, so much so that they 'truly believe that the things that make them less efficient than sharks or robots are weaknesses'.[50]

That's why unionism matters. A major labour struggle dispels the moral authority of the employer, encouraging workers to think about the evils that the everyday tyranny of the workplace facilitates — including the environmental destruction it enables.

There's nothing inevitable about that process. The Green Bans depended on a unique set of people and politics, one that won't be easily recreated. Industrial struggle isn't a magical solution. There's no workplace wand that conjures away the difficulties we face. As Sarah Jaffe says, 'labor ... is us: messy, desiring, hungry, lonely, angry, frustrated human beings.'[51] We are not always defiant at work. We don't always rebel.

Sometimes, however, we do — and the consequences can be profound.

CHAPTER THIRTEEN

News from Somewhere

A tree-filled city on the banks of a crystalline river in which salmon splash. Orchards surrounding a parliament house now used to store manure. Workers reacquainted with the land, so that the 'world of the country vivified by the thought and briskness of town-bred folk [produces a] happy and leisurely but eager life'. Children encouraged to study the wild creatures about them, learning by playing in forests. A nation resembling 'a garden, where nothing is wasted and nothing is spoilt, with the necessary dwellings, sheds and workshops scattered up and down the country ...'

That's how the nineteenth-century poet, artist, and activist William Morris imagined a future London: a socialist paradise, but also manifestly an environmental one.[1]

Morris wrote his book *News from Nowhere* in the midst of an explosion of utopian fiction in the 1890s, a decade in which theorists of all persuasions used literature to develop visions of better worlds. Amidst the deprivations and inequalities of the late-Victorian age, activists struggled not with an absence of hope, but a surfeit of it. Rather than concluding that change was impossible, they confronted a plethora of futures, with advocates of particular improvements striving to distinguish their schemas from those of their rivals.

That's not the situation today. Despite the wonder of our technologies, we have lost the capacity for utopia. In the twenty-first century, we remain unable to imagine a coherent alternative to a capitalist system that is, quite literally, killing us.

Way back in the 1920s, researchers William F Ogburn and Dorothy S Thomas noted that human mortality actually increased during economic booms. '[I]n both England and the USA,' Thomas subsequently explained, 'a high death rate is associated with periods of prosperity and a low death rate with periods of [economic] depression.'[2] This bizarre and counter-intuitive finding has repeatedly been confirmed ever since, most recently with a study of twenty-three countries during the Global Financial Crisis.[3]

It's not that recessions do us good. It's more that economic growth means that we smoke and drink more, we sleep and exercise less, and we spend our time in dangerous industrial settings.[4] Nevertheless, our entire political culture centres around increasing GDP, which benefits capital and makes our lives demonstrably worse. We obsess about blind economic growth — and that growth kills us.

In his book *Capitalist Realism*, Mark Fisher diagnoses the dominance of a 'business ontology', a mentality that can only conceive of human activities insofar as they're profitable.[5] For instance, researchers associated with the International Monetary Fund (IMF) recently noted that whales — especially great whales — capture from the atmosphere considerable amounts of carbon, which they store in their huge bodies and take down to the ocean floor when they die. A single great whale can thus sequester 33 tons of carbon dioxide — a not-insignificant quantity, given that a tree only absorbs 48 pounds annually. Whales also feed populations of phytoplankton with their waste, and, globally, those phytoplankton capture some 37 billion metric tons of carbon dioxide, four times the emissions sequestered by the jungles of the Amazon.[6]

Whales, in other words, protect our climate. That makes their continuing decline a threat to the planet — and a warning about how one industrial process (such as whaling) can exacerbate the effects of another (the fossil-fuel industry) in unexpected and disastrous ways.

But that isn't the IMF's conclusion. For its researchers, the relationship between whales and carbon establishes merely that the creatures must be commodified. Once priced — the IMF estimates each whale as worth about $2 million— they could be enlisted in a market constructed to compensate those countries, businesses, and individuals otherwise financially invested in their extinction. Indeed, the IMF and the World Bank are, we are told, already 'well placed to help governments integrate the macroeconomic benefit that whales provide in mitigating climate change, as well as the cost of measures to protect the whales, into their macro-fiscal frameworks'.[7]

The IMF's paper simply assumes that, without price signals, people will exterminate whales, with human behaviour determined by rational profit maximisation and nothing else. It treats markets as more natural than nature itself; it considers the ocean's inability to evolve an adequate pricing measure a failing that benevolent economists must carefully amend.

Such is the profound strangeness of our current moment, a strangeness that often escapes our recognition. If you or I encountered a whale stranded on the beach, we wouldn't construct a market to reward its potential saviour. We would do our best to push it back into the sea. Why don't we adopt the same approach to the environment as a whole? Why not democratically and rationally decide the measures needed to save the planet, and then ... do them?

For the vast bulk of human history, production has taken place within a web of social relations, dominated by principles such as reciprocity, redistribution, and use. In the ancient world or under feudalism, decisions about what was made might not have been democratic but they were unquestionably *decisions*, deliberate choices taken by people, with markets only a distinctly secondary consideration.[8]

By contrast, the most fundamental aspects of our behaviour are now determined by forces we experience as entirely beyond our control.

It was this realisation that turned William Morris into a socialist.

In the 1870s, Morris was already a beloved public figure, acclaimed throughout Britain as an artist, designer, and writer. His design firm, Morris and Co., was both successful and fashionable; *The Times* called him 'one of our half dozen best poets'.

When he formed the Society for the Preservation of Ancient Buildings in 1877, his opposition to the ugly, shoddy architecture reshaping England's cities might have remained the harmless hobby of a gentleman aesthete. Instead, his love for the structures of the past led Morris, relatively late in his career, into radical politics, simply because he grasped that the desecration of heritage stemmed not from bad decisions, but from the imperatives of capitalism— what he called 'the present conditions of a sordid and heart-breaking struggle for existence for the many, and a languid sauntering through life for the few'.[9]

The technical advances of the nineteenth century should have meant better places in which to work and to live, workshops and homes that artfully used technology in ways that the people of the past could not have imagined. Instead, Morris realised, the pursuit of profit was 'surely and not slowly destroying the beauty of the very face of the earth'.[10] His concern for the urban landscape led him, like the New South Wales Builders Labourers Federation a hundred years later, into a recognisable form of environmentalism — and, like the leaders of the BLF, he came to argue for the replacement of capitalism with a planned socialist economy.

Today, planning has been discredited by association with the

Soviet Union and the grey and vicious dictatorships of the Eastern bloc. It's dismissed as utopian by the people who advocate market fantasies such as whale pricing.

Yet entirely the wrong lessons have been absorbed from the USSR and the experience of the twentieth century. Planning needn't be some wild dream. Even today, it's a fundamental part of everyday capitalism. Every giant corporation sets quotas, makes projections, and establishes strategies. It does so precisely because of competition. Each CEO knows she must guide her company's allocation of resources because, if she doesn't, her more far-sighted competitors will seize the initiative.

Stalinist planning was not so different. The Soviet Union needed to outproduce its Western rivals — and that imperative shaped the command economy through which the USSR industrialised at breakneck speed. The Stalinist bureaucrats established their five-year plans to compete militarily and economically with Western Europe and the United States, and that competition compelled them to adopt the expansionist dynamic of capitalism.

Obviously, in the Soviet Union, planning wasn't democratic. On the contrary, a small number of men devised the plans to which the rest of the nation were subjected. For most Soviet citizens, economic planning simply meant quotas imposed by their bosses. Not surprisingly, workers sought to resist the resulting speed-ups and overtime, even as managers threatened them with punishments.

Anyone who has worked for a big organisation will empathise. External competition might necessitate internal planning, but rigid corporate hierarchies leave CEOs out of touch with the day-to-day workings of their organisations. As a result, their strategies often appear to ordinary employees as arbitrary — and often unpleasant or tedious — directives. The head of a multinational company can't send you to a gulag — but behind her commands lies the threat of dismissal, which only makes you resent the company plan more.

None of this is new, of course. William Morris developed his ideas on socialism explicitly in opposition to the kind of top-down diktats we now associate with planning. He wrote *News from Nowhere* as a direct response to the American journalist Edward Bellamy, who had published his own novel, *Looking Backward,* in 1888.[11]

In that book, Bellamy's protagonist, Julian West, falls into a long hypnotic trance, waking in the year 2000 to discover that the enormous trusts of the nineteenth century have been nationalised. Collectivisation has transformed society into a state-directed 'machine ... so logical in its principles and direct and simple in its workings that it all but runs itself'.[12] In this new world, all citizens must enlist in a disciplined 'industrial army', though the system's efficiency means they can retire at forty-five and thereafter enjoy a life of leisure.

Even though the book intended to popularise socialism, Bellamy's depiction appalled Morris. For him, *Looking Backward* portrayed not freedom, but an intensification of the bureaucratic compulsion that already marred nineteenth-century society. Rather than a utopia, Morris saw Bellamy as offering only a 'huge national centralization, working by a kind of magic for which no one feels himself responsible'.[13]

He wrote *News from Nowhere* in 1890 to distinguish from Bellamy his own vision of what he dubbed 'an undegraded existence on the earth'.[14]

Morris's novel replicates the basic structure of *Looking Backward* (and the utopian genre as a whole), with a nineteenth-century man (known as 'Guest') awakening in the future to learn, via Socratic dialogues with helpful citizens, how the new socialist Britain functions. But whereas Bellamy describes a militarised industry benignly directed by a 'group of men at Washington', *News from Nowhere* portrays communes of ordinary men and women making their own decisions about how, where, and why they work.

It depicts socialist England as integrated into a socialist world, so that its citizens aren't forced to outcompete with military rivals elsewhere. The people directly control the fields and the factories, and, because of that, they can produce for human use rather than capitalist profit. They make and grow what they need; they've stopped pumping out what they don't require.

Far more than most socialists in the nineteenth century — and many in the twentieth — Morris illustrates the environmental possibilities of planning. Guest marvels, for instance, at how London's chimneys no longer belch smoke, and at how the polluting soap factories and toxic leadworks have vanished. The citizens, he discovers, have collectively decided to reorganise such industries, eschewing some products and making others through different means. Without the requirement to chase profit, they can decide what matters to them, not to the market.

A comparable freedom today would enable all manner of currently impossible responses to the ecological disasters we confront. Most obviously, we could do something unimaginable under capitalism — we could stop. We could pull the emergency brake on the runaway train, directly and immediately ceasing the practices we know to be destroying the climate, without having to wait for the market to decide that no further profits can be wrung from coal. We could instead devote our massive resources and technological capabilities to staunching the wounds already inflicted on the planet.

Each year, the world spends over $1,917 billion on guns, bombs, and other military equipment.[15] The comparable figure on advertising is some $325 billion.[16] Those staggering figures represent a mere fraction of what we could direct immediately to environmental programs on land, sea, and air. We could begin systemic decarbonisation, closing down coal-fired power stations, and replacing fossil fuels with electricity from renewables such as solar, using the process to reduce rather than increase our energy needs. We could massively expand low-carbon public transport, so that efficient, easy-to-use, and convenient electric trains and trams replaced internal-combustion engines. We could replan our cities and towns for human convenience rather than for the use of automobiles; we could establish methods of recycling and re-use that genuinely reduced material throughputs.[17]

Even formulating that list makes one weep with frustration. We know what's required and yet, all along the line, we're impeded by the imperatives of capital and the insistence on blind, mathematical, destructive growth. Hence Naomi Klein's anguished recognition that 'a serious response to the climate threat involves recovering an art that has been relentlessly vilified ... planning. Lots and lots of planning.'[18]

A planned economy offers an alternative: a fundamentally different way to respond to environmental crisis. But can socialist planning actually work, or should we dismiss *News from Nowhere* as merely the pleasant dream of an eccentric poet?

Defenders of the free market tell us that aspirations to democratise the economy must inevitably founder on the complexity of globalisation. Every day, they say, trillions of independent price signals come together at the cash register to enable the co-ordination of production all around the world. No mortals could replicate that superhuman efficiency, and any attempt to do so would lead to stifling bureaucracy. The cheery villagers who Guest meets might be able to decide collectively on constructing a bridge over their local brook, but they could not cope with the demands of a sophisticated twenty-first–century nation: in real life, the argument goes, their efforts at democratic planning would necessarily foster centralised dictatorship.

Now, such claims about capitalist co-ordination always rest on idealisations of the market, rather than on the sclerotic and dysfunctional institution that governs us in the real world. Actually existing capitalism does not smoothly allocate resources, but oscillates between slumps and booms, generating both fantastical surpluses and appalling shortages. The environmental crisis is, in and of itself, a sufficient rebuttal of the system's efficiency — even before we consider that, each year, the industrialised nations waste $680 billion worth of food and let 690 million people starve.[19]

Nevertheless, it's true that modern societies are fearsomely complex. For that reason, a planned economy would, indeed, require central co-ordination at the national and international level — something to which Morris doesn't give adequate attention. But that co-ordination wouldn't mean a Stalinist central committee or, for that matter, a boardroom full of high-flying CEOs. There is no necessary incompatibility between planning and, say, an electoral system by which delegates are selected to a national governance body.

A peak democratic body could plan by consulting relevant experts, assessing the various proposals they put forward, and then deciding upon the nation's overarching priorities. It could determine the broad distribution of resources and the importance of different productive sectors. It could establish the prices of goods and services to reflect the relative costs associated with their production, and the scarcity or abundance of materials they require; and could monitor progress towards previously set objectives, adjusting targets as necessary.[20]

Yet, within that general context, the decentralised decision-making Morris describes would remain crucial, with local production collectives, consumer bodies, and neighbourhood groups choosing for themselves how best to fulfil those aspects of the plan for which they were most responsible.

Consider Britain during the Second World War, a period in which a war cabinet essentially took charge of the entire economy and directed it to the achievement of victory. During that time, the government did not establish a single overall blueprint. Instead, it decided on general priorities and rough plans for different economic sectors, which were then constantly updated by a process of approximation and negotiation with those responsible for their implementation. Though the economy was mostly geared to heavy industry, the resources reserved for civil consumption were distributed 'through consumer surveys and by watching statistics of stocks and sales [...] with production [...] then organised to meet demand'.[21]

The system worked, facilitating a remarkable — and remarkably rapid — transition from peacetime conditions to a war economy. In 1938, for instance, Britain had allocated 7.4 per cent of national expenditure to rearmament — and, five years later, that figure had shot up to 55.3 per cent. At the height of the conflict, something like half the working population was engaged in the armed forces, the munitions industries, or other fields essential to the war effort.[22] As one observer noted, 'the power to make rapid changes in the disposition of the nation's resources was the greatest war-winning weapon of all'.[23]

The unbridled authority enjoyed by the British state at that time led the environmental scientist James Lovelock to propose, in his 2009 book *The Vanishing Face of Gaia,* the temporary suspension of democratic government so as to allow a Second World War-style emergency climate intervention.[24]

But Lovelock totally misunderstood what made wartime planning possible. The system worked despite and not because of authoritarianism. As Pat Devine argues, its success depended on two central factors: first, the active support of the population, and, second, the provision of adequate information to the planners.[25]

These were, of course, intimately connected. Despite the privations of the war, the commitment of ordinary people to the defeat of the Nazis meant that, by and large, they accepted government priorities, and they spoke honestly about how and where plans required adjustment. The men and women on the shopfloor wanted the economy to succeed; they used their intimate knowledge of each factory to see that it did.

A planned economy does not need military discipline. On the contrary, it relies on a new and much greater freedom — as William Morris recognised.

Unlike many intellectuals, Morris knew something of physical work. Morris's biographer EP Thompson notes his mastery of glass firing, tile glazing, embroidery, woodcutting, engraving, pottery, bookbinding, weaving, and many other industrial skills. His practical appreciation of artisanal production shaped his understanding of socialist planning.[26]

Work, Morris insisted, was not innately hateful. On the contrary, humans possessed an inescapable need to reshape their world. Labour wasn't an optional extra, but an activity that defined us as a species, something as necessary to us as breathing. To live, we manipulated nature, and we tended to enjoy doing it well.

For Morris, that human 'joy in labour' was an aesthetic sensation. 'The chief source of art,' Morris said, 'is man's pleasure in his daily necessary work, which expresses itself and is embodied in that work itself.'[27]

Wage labour, however, transformed our relationship with nature into meaningless drudgery, an activity controlled not by us but by the imperatives of impersonal profit. Even if we want to express ourselves in beautiful work, we cannot: the system compels us to toil as directed, creating exchange values rather than working for purposes significant to us.

In *News from Nowhere*, Morris thus describes a society in which labour power no longer serves as a commodity, one in which workers consciously and democratically create objects and provide services to meet human needs. People control their own activity, and that production for use cuts waste and increases productivity, because it also changes the subjective experience of labour. Rather than hating work, they fear a potential shortage of it, because, as one of Guest's new friends explains:

> *All* work is now pleasurable; either because of the hope of gain in honour and wealth with which the work is done, which causes pleasurable excitement, even when the actual work is not pleasant; or else because it has grown into a pleasurable *habit*, as in the case with what you may call mechanical work; and lastly (and most of our work is of this kind) because there is conscious sensuous pleasure in the work itself; it is done, that is, by artists.[28]

That sounds like pure fantasy, so let's take a step back and tease out what Morris means.

At the simplest level, he's suggesting that even horrible, tedious jobs possess a different character depending on the circumstances under which we perform them. Plenty of people who wouldn't want to change sewer systems all day still spend their holidays tinkering with the pipes in their bush shack.

If we understood why we performed the work we did; if we could see that our daily tasks contributed, in an immediate and meaningful way, to making life better for our community; and if we felt we had genuine influence over decisions in our workplaces, we might feel, in our labour, the same satisfaction we currently receive from our hobbies.

In any case, a planned economy could eliminate many unpleasant or dangerous jobs, simply by taking into account the human consequences of production. If your factories don't generate toxic sludge, no one has to spend their days as a sludge-remover. Similarly, automaton might be deployed to end drudgery, in ways that capitalism finds impossible. As the characters in *News from Nowhere* explain to Guest, the democratic control of the industrial process means machines become servants rather than masters. Instead of technology making meaningful labour tedious, it can be deployed to free people from odious or hazardous tasks. At the same time, if handicraft offers a more beautiful or satisfying result, the machines can be switched off.

Economists insist that humans work only for personal enrichment. We're rational profit-maximisers, they say, stirred from our innate laziness by the prospect of individual gain. But they're describing a capitalist logic, not a human one. Since the 1940s, behaviourists have shown repeatedly that people crave challenges. If they need wages to eat, they'll labour for wages. But as the psychologist Edward Deci showed in a series of famous experiments in 1969, external rewards actually dull enthusiasm for a task, almost certainly because they're generally linked to an absence of control. His subjects showed far more interest when they could learn, explore, exercise their skills, and extend themselves. That was when they really tried.[29]

Morris's comparison between labour and art doesn't, after all, mean that labour can't be arduous or difficult. If anything, it implies the opposite. George Orwell once described writing a book as 'a horrible, exhausting struggle, like a long bout with some painful illness', and suggested that no one would do such thing unless compelled by a demonic force they could not resist.[30] Writing, like other forms of art, is agonising. Nevertheless, it feels profoundly meaningful to the writer — so much so that Orwell pushed himself to complete a novel even as he was dying of tuberculosis.

Morris saw art as a form of labour. It emerged from humanity's relationship to nature, a result of our necessary engagement with the natural world. Genuine aesthetic achievement depends on human freedom, for without that we could not feel joy in our toil, our connection with nature. But that also means art provides a glimpse of what work could become. We might say that, where Stalin describes artists as engineers of the human soul, Morris recognises human art as the soul of engineering, since he understands artistic creation as a model for the world's transformation.

In the society he describes, aesthetic satisfaction from the sensuous activity of labour changes people's relationship with the world, with each other, and with themselves. They now work with — rather than on or against — nature, consciously integrating their activities into the cycles of land, animals, and plants.

For instance, Guest meets a woman called Clara, who ponders the ecological devastation caused by people of the nineteenth century:

> Was not their mistake once more bred of the life of slavery that they had been living? — a life which was always looking upon everything, except mankind, animate and inanimate — 'nature,' as people used to call it — as one thing, and mankind as another, it was natural to people thinking in this way, that they should try to make 'nature' their slave, since they thought 'nature' was something outside them.[31]

Clara, by contrast, doesn't see nature as external to humanity, because the control she exerts over her labour directly connects her to the objects she works with, reminding her constantly that people are as inseparable from their environment as fish are from water.

Yet the democratic power that she and her fellows exert over their daily lives does not conflict with the central planning upon which the whole system depends. As economist David Laibman explains:

> Put simply: good, effective central coordination is a precondition
> for good, effective decentral coordination, and vice versa. The
> mutual necessities are clear: the central level provides stability
> and visibility — prices, norms, general structural conditions
> determining needs for and sources of goods. This stable
> framework enables decentral units to calculate, compare, act.[32]

Local democracy enables central planning, and vice versa. Because people shape their own lives, they develop their capacities and extend their horizons. Production for use doesn't merely facilitate the creation of material possessions. It also creates citizens who are rich in interests, enthusiasms, and ambitions — and as such have both the desire and capability to control their own society.[33]

Morris's enthusiasm for forests, rivers, and fields means that even admirers often dismiss *News from Nowhere* as a bucolic fantasy. Yet, as John Bellamy Foster argues, Morris didn't argue for a return to nature so much as 'the return of nature and ... unalienated human values', based on the rejection of the distortions engendered by capitalism.[34]

Morris wrote *News from Nowhere* as a novel, not as an economics text. It doesn't provide enthusiasts for the society of the future with a plan to follow. Then again, if we're genuine in our commitment to popular democracy, blueprints are innately problematic, since they impose on the people of tomorrow plans we've devised for them today. It's more useful to extrapolate from our understanding of the present to the conditions upon which a different order might be built.

Obviously, that's no easy task, and the brief sketch I've provided leaves more questions unanswered than resolved. How might we abandon the anarchy of the market, given the likely resistance from those with an interest in the status quo? Given the destruction already wreaked on the planet, what elements of consumer culture might be salvaged as we wrestle with the simultaneous imperatives to decarbonise and provide decent lives for those in the nations least responsible for carbon emissions? How might our cities be re-imagined? What can we do about agriculture, about air travel, about non-renewable resources?

These and many other problems will only be solved through prolonged debates, drawing on the lessons of history as well a process of practical trial and error. Nothing about that will be easy.

But the future also speaks to the present.

At the end of *News from Nowhere*, Guest finds himself awakening back in his own day, and fears, for a terrible instant, that he's dreamed the whole encounter. That's why he resolves to tell his story. For, as he explains in the novel's final words, 'if others can see it as I have seen it, then it may be called a vision rather than a dream'.[35]

As Morris knew, if we don't believe that the world might be different, we're stuck with the world as it is. If we can't imagine a fairer society, we can't protest injustice. A democratic and planned economy offers us an alternative model of what life might be like — and thus a banner under which to fight today.

Make Hope Great Again

In the 1940s, Aldo Leopold mused on how an environmental consciousness meant realising you were living in a 'world of wounds'. Back then, one needed an ecological education to see the planet's bruises.

Today, it's impossible to avoid them.

Precisely because we face a crisis existential in its implications, minimal programs fail to inspire. We all know, deep in our guts, that we won't get out of this without massive change. The cautious, 'sensible' proposals put forward by politicians don't inspire anyone. Perversely, they seem utopian: a fantasy of moderation in which no one really believes.

Atmospheric physics doesn't care about good intentions; the melting glaciers won't make any allowances for political realities and the art of the possible. Conventional pragmatism does not suit environmental crises. Either we will do what's required, or we won't. There are no half-measures. Rather than asking what's realistic and then pretending it's what we need, we should recognise what's required and then plan to make it possible.

Capitalism will kill the planet. It must be replaced. That sounds daunting. It *is* daunting — and it would be foolish to pretend otherwise. Nevertheless, there are reasons for hope.

If there's any certainty about what lies ahead, it's that the future won't be like the past. We're living through a time of transformation. In an already intensifying crisis, each month normalises events that, just a few years previously, would have been considered entirely fanciful. Consider Donald Trump, a president so unlikely that he once featured as a gag on *The Simpsons*. Who imagined the world's only superpower led by a reality-show huckster, a man willing to cheer on a crowd of conspiracy theorists and white nationalists as they fought their way into the Capitol building? Or think about Covid-19 and the manner in which, almost overnight, it upended political realities so thoroughly that conservative politicians implemented welfare schemes far more radical than anything proposed by mainstream social democrats.

Without question, change looms. What that change looks like depends on us. Amidst such uncertainty, we can't draw up plans to be followed. We can, however, identify some basic principles for what lies ahead.

Be suspicious of the inevitable attempts to blame crises on ordinary people. We've been subjected to those arguments for decades, and many of us have internalised them. We all have some unlearning to do. Progressives can become frustrated at the aching slowness of action, and take comfort in belittling the supposedly brainwashed dupes in the suburbs. But next time you hear someone — whether a politician, a journalist, or an activist — dismissing the masses as stupid, lazy, and greedy, ask yourself what follows from that rhetoric. Who benefits from victim-blaming? Why are so many powerful figures so determined to portray humanity as worthless? If environmental slogans don't resonate, ask what's wrong with the slogans. How might you present the case for a better world in ways that mean something to your friends, neighbours, and workmates?

Don't be guilt-tripped into supposed solutions based entirely

on personal responsibility. No doubt, in the decades to come, we'll all have to make sacrifices. But we're not going to end global heating by choosing greener brands or measuring carbon footprints. Live an ethical life as much as you can. But recognise that for you — and for everyone else — the possibilities for moral choices are circumscribed by barriers not of your making. Within the limits of capitalism, your options are scarce. Pretending otherwise makes you unhappy, and distracts you from the real sources of that unhappiness.

Recognise and oppose those supposedly environmental interventions that merely advance the interests of capital. As the crises worsen, greenwashing will become more prevalent and more ubiquitous. Corporations are not our friends and do not mean us well, no matter how many green commodities they peddle.

Learn to argue. Part of respecting ordinary men and women is believing them capable of persuasion. If it's wrong to dismiss working people as innately venal, it's equally wrong to nod along with bad ideas just because they're popular. There's no greater respect you can show someone than trying to change their mind. Listen to others. Be prepared to learn. Be fair and open-minded — but fight like hell for what you know to be right.

Expect opposition. If you attribute the environmental crisis to the carcinogenic expansion of capitalism, you're pointing your finger at the most powerful people who have ever lived. They will not thank you for doing so. Environmentalists who rail against overpopulation or urge us to use keep cups mostly receive genial toleration, precisely because they don't threaten powerful interests. But those who blame capitalism face ridicule when they're weak, and much worse when they're strong.

Find collective projects to join and support. Nothing changes without organisation. You can't know in advance what forms struggles will take. But the campaigns, groups, and parties that really matter will be organised from the bottom up. They will be loud and messy and strident. They will be denounced by politicians, and will spark controversy in the media. But they will involve ordinary people raising their own voices and acting on their own behalf.

Organise at work. Join your union. Talk to your workmates. Find out what matters to them and what they'd like to change. Any effort, no matter how prosaic, to exert power at work alters the way people think about who they are and what they do. Look out for openings, big or small, to connect working life with the wider world in which that work takes place.

Organise wherever else you might be. If you're at school or university, join a club or set one up. Speak to your neighbours about local issues. Get your social media friends interested in real-world activities.

Democratise everything. In theory, our leaders all love democracy. In practice, they respond to it like the devil to holy water. In a commodified world, there's no more radical idea than that ordinary people should not merely be surveyed or counselled, but should actually decide. Democracy needn't be an empty abstraction. It's good to talk about making parliament democratic; it's better to push democracy in our schools, our workplaces, our communities, our unions, and our campaigns.

Make connections. The problems we face are systemic, and so the struggles against them can support each other. A union campaign for a wage rise will not save the polar bears. But in a confident, unionised workplace, it's much easier to raise environmental issues. The unity we require to build a new world leaves no room for racism or sexism. If you call them out when you see them, you make climate organising easier.

Prepare to be unprepared. The Bible warns that the Lord will come like a thief in the night. In a world of crisis, we can't know exactly what will propel the next major struggle. Almost certainly, it won't take the form that we were expecting. Throughout history, you can find examples of long-time radicals wrongfooted by sudden change. Don't let the past blind you to the potential of the future.

Stay hopeful. The current economic, social, and environmental instability almost guarantees the development of some kind of radicalism. It may well be the radicalism of the far right — in fact, it almost certainly will be, unless and until progressives make hope great again.

That's why history matters. It matters, for instance, that Indigenous people lived for tens of thousands of years in ways that fostered rather than degraded nature. From the technological world of the twenty-first century, we cannot, of course, return to the conditions that prevailed in a pre-1788 Australia. But that's not the point. The remarkably rapid destruction of the landscape created by Indigenous people was not brought about by modern machines. On the contrary, the settlers ruined the land with distinctly low-tech methods (such as running cattle and building fences). The problem was not technology, but a social system that deployed technology in certain ways, replacing the conscious choices of humans with the blind agency of capital.

The implications of this cannot be stressed enough. If it's possible (and we know it is) for humans to enhance rather than strangle nature — if we can tend and nourish the world outside us — then we needn't accept a gradual degradation of the planet as our best-case scenario.

Even now, in these desperate times, environmentalism could be something other than a desperate rearguard action, more than an impossible effort to preserve a wilderness in peril from our very existence. We could offer a real program of redemption, one that made the planet better rather than just less bad.[1]

In the midst of crisis, we can easily forget the wondrous accomplishments of which humans are capable. We can send a rover to Mars; we can identify dinosaur DNA; we can grow artificial meat in laboratories. It's preposterous to think we cannot change how we relate to each other and to the natural world.

Percy Shelley wrote 'The Mask of Anarchy', one of the greatest poems of resistance, at a time when industrial capitalism was still new. In it, he condemns the men responsible for the Peterloo Massacre, an incident in which British cavalry charged protesters agitating for democratic reform in Manchester.

He names, in particular, Robert Stewart (Lord Castlereagh), the Leader of the House of Commons, writing:

I met Murder on the way –
He had a mask like Castlereagh –
Very smooth he looked, yet grim …

As we have seen, many of the businesses most responsible for global warming proved decades ago to their own satisfaction that carbon dioxide could affect the climate in catastrophic ways — and yet they continued normal operations regardless.

That's murder — social murder — on a scale beyond anything Castlereagh could have imagined. Yet the smooth, grim people destroying our planet remain a tiny minority. The American Climate Accountability Institute recently emphasised that some twenty fossil-fuel companies can be linked directly to more than one-third of greenhouse-gas emissions in the modern era.[2]

Is it really beyond our capabilities to defeat this evil clique?

Shelley concludes 'The Mask of Anarchy' by urging his readers to realise their power:

Shake your chains to earth like dew,
Which in sleep had fallen on you –
Ye are many — they are few.[3]

The words could not be more relevant today.

Acknowledgements

This project was assisted by the Cultural Fund of the Copyright Agency. Thank you to Nicola Evans and all the staff there. Thank you to everyone who commented on the manuscript, particularly Michael Pulsford, Gary Pearce, Martin Empson, Petra Stock, Kulja Coulston, Alex Ettling, Mathew Abbott, Stephanie Convery, and everyone in the Red-Green Reading Group. Some of this material appeared in different forms in other places — thank you to editors at *Overland*, the *Guardian*, *Counterpunch*, and elsewhere. Thank you to my agent Martin Shaw, to Teresa Goudie, and to Henry Rosenbloom and everyone at Scribe.

Notes

Introduction: The Guilty Party

1   The attribution may be apocryphal.
2   Larry Elliot, 'World's 26 richest people own as much as poorest 50%, says Oxfam', *The Guardian*, 21 May 2019.

Chapter One: The Hydrocarbon Explosion Engine

A version of this argument appeared in *Overland* 236, spring 2019, under the title 'The Great Acceleration'.

1   Denis Leary, *Asshole*, 1995.
2   Nadine Unger, Tami C Bond, James S Wang, Dorothy M Koch, Surabi Menon, Drew T Shindell, and Susanne Bauer, 'Attribution of Climate Forcing to Economic Sectors', *Proceedings of the National Academy of Sciences*, 107.8 (2010), pp 3382–87.
3   'Number of Vehicles in Operation in the United States Between 3rd quarter 2016 and 3rd quarter 2020 (in millions)' in *Statista*, <https://www.statista.com/statistics/859950/vehicles-in-operation-by-quarter-united-states/>
4   Catherine Lutz and Anne Lutz Fernandez, *Carjacked: the culture of the automobile and its effect on our lives* (New York: St. Martin's Press, 2010), p 9.
5   Robert Ferris, 'China Annual Auto Sales Fall for First Time in about Two Decades', *CNBC*, 3 January 2019.
6   Samuel Chamberlain, 'Trump Mocks Green New Deal, Pokes Fun at Electric Cars during Michigan Rally' *Fox News,* 28 March 2019.
7   Elaine L Chao and Andrew Wheeler, 'Make Cars Great Again', *Wall Street Journal*, 2 August 2018.

8   Peter Norton, 'Of Love Affairs and Other Stories' in Stephen Zavestoski and Julian Agyeman, eds., *Incomplete Streets: processes, practices and possibilities* (Abingdom & New York, Routledge, 2015), p 17.

9   André Gorz, 'The Social Ideology of the Motorcar', *Uneven Earth*, 11 August 2018.

10 Daniel Marc Albert, *Are We There Yet?: the American automobile, past, present, and driverless* (New York: Norton & Company, 2019), p 20.

11 Norton, p 21.

12 Peter Norton, *Fighting Traffic: the dawn of the motor age in the American city* (Cambridge: MIT Press, 2008), p 24.

13 Edward Humes, 'The Absurd Primacy of the Automobile in American Life', *Atlantic*, 12 April 2016.

14 Tom McCarthy, *Auto Mania: cars, consumers, and the environment* (New Haven: Yale University Press, 2007), p 13.

15 Albert, p 12.

16 McCarthy, p 11.

17 Norton, *Fighting Traffic*, p 23.

18 Joseph Stromberg, 'The Forgotten History of How Automakers Invented the Crime of "Jaywalking"', *Vox*, 4 November 2015.

19 Albert, p 18.

20 Albert, p 26.

21 Edwin Black, *Internal Combustion: how corporations and governments addicted the world to oil and derailed the alternatives* (London: St. Martin's Press, 2006), p 64.

22 David A Kirsch, 'The Electric Car and the Burden of History: studies in automotive systems rivalry in America, 1890–1996', *Business and Economic History*, 26.2 (1997), p 307.

23 Albert, p 31.

24 Christophe Bonneuil and Jean-Baptiste Fressoz, *The Shock of the Anthropocene: the Earth, history, and us* (London: Verso ebook, 2016), Chapter Five.

25 Norton, *Fighting Traffic*, p 24.

26 Norton, *Fighting Traffic*, p 23.

27 Brian Addison, 'The (Classist, Racist) History of Jaywalking', *CounterPunch*, 13 March 2018.

28 Ravi Mangla, 'The Secret History of Jaywalking: the disturbing reason it was outlawed — and why we should lift the ban', *Salon*, 21 August 2015.

29 Norton, *Fighting Traffic*, p 25.

30 Albert, p 25.

31 Lutz and Fernandez, p 9.

32 Bonneuil and Fressoz, Chapter Seven.

33 Gorz.

34 Norton, *Fighting Traffic*, p 173.

35 Raymond Williams, *Raymond Williams on Culture & Society: essential writings* (Los Angeles: SAGE, 2014), p 144.

36 Gorz.

37 Tom Vanderbilt, 'How Not Having a Car Became Hollywood Shorthand for Loser', *Salon,* 30 July 2010.

38 Gerardo Marletto, *Structure, Agency and Change in The Car Regime: a review of the literature*, Working Papers (Rome: CREI Università degli Studi Roma Tre, 2010), p 7.

39 Black, p 64.

Chapter Two: Farewell to Sudan

1 Anne Sexton, 'The Earth Falls Down' in *The Awful Rowing Toward God* (Boston: Houghton Mifflin, 1975), p 14.

2 Sexton, p 14.

3 George Perkins Marsh, *Man and Nature; Or, Physical Geography as Modified by Human Action* (New York: Charles Scribner, 1867), p 36.

4 Joseph R McConnell, Andrew I Wilson, Andreas Stohl, Monica M Arienzo, Nathan J Chellman, Sabine Eckhardt, Elisabeth M Thompson, A Mark Pollard, and Jørgen Peder Steffensen, 'Lead Pollution Recorded in Greenland Ice Indicates European Emissions Tracked Plagues, Wars, and Imperial Expansion During Antiquity',

Proceedings of the National Academy of Sciences, 115.22, May 2018, pp 5726–31.

5   Lucas Stephens, Erle Ellis, and Dorian Fuller, 'Revolutionary Archaeology Reveals the Deepest Possible Anthropocene, *Aeon*, 1 October 2020.

6   Joris PGM Cromsigt and Mariska te Beest, 'Restoration of a Megaherbivore: landscape-level impacts of white rhinoceros in Kruger National Park, South Africa', *Journal of Ecology*, 102.3 (2014), pp 566–75; Matthew Waldram, 'The Ecological Effects of Grazing by the White Rhino (Ceratotherium Simum Simum) at a Landscape Scale', Masters thesis, University of Cape Town, 2005.

7   Mark S Boyce, 'Wolves for Yellowstone: dynamics in time and space', *Journal of Mammalogy*, 99.5 (2018), pp 1021–31.

8   Marsh, p 4.

9   Marvin Perry, *Sources of the Western Tradition, Volume 1* (Boston: Cengage Learning, 2012), p 113.

10   Bryan Christy, 'Inside the Deadly Rhino Horn Trade', *National Geographic*, 6 October 2016.

Chapter Three: The Earth Glows No More Divine

1   Alexander Koch, Chris Brierley, Mark M Maslin, and Simon L Lewis, 'Earth System Impacts of the European Arrival and Great Dying in the Americas after 1492', *Quaternary Science Reviews*, 207 (2019), pp 13–36.

2   Philipp Blom, *Nature's Mutiny: how the little ice age of the long seventeenth century transformed the West and shaped the present* (New York: WW Norton & Company, 2019), p 17.

3   Alan Frost, 'New South Wales as *Terra Nullius*: the British denial of Aboriginal land rights', *Historical Studies*, 19.77 (1981), p 520.

4   Bill Gammage, *The Biggest Estate on Earth: how Aborigines made Australia* (Melbourne: Allen & Unwin, 2011), p 43.

5   Gammage, p 8.

6   Henry Reynolds, *The Other Side of the Frontier: Aboriginal resistance*

to the European invasion of Australia (Sydney: University of New South Wales Press, 1981), p 144.

7   James Boyce, *1835: the founding of Melbourne and the conquest of Australia* (Melbourne: Black Inc, 2011), p 339.

8   Boyce, p 282.

9   Bruce Pascoe, *Dark Emu: black seeds, agriculture or accident?* (Broome: Magabala Books, 2014), p 9.

10 Ross Gittins, 'Maybe the colonialists were actually a minority', *The Age*, 26 December 2015.

11 Cited in Melissa Lucashenko, 'The First Australian Democracy', *Meanjin*, 74.3 (2015), p 10.

12 Cited in Lucashenko, p 8.

13 Eleanor Burke Leacock, *Myths of Male Dominance: collected articles on women cross-culturally* (Chicago: Haymarket Books, 2008), p 21.

14 Elizabeth Humphrys, 'The Birth of Australia: non-capitalist social relations in a capitalist mode of production?', *Journal of Australian Political Economy*, 70 (Summer 2012–13), pp 110–29.

15 Ben Hillier and Tom O'Lincoln, 'Five Hundred Lashes and Double Irons: the origins of Australian capitalism', *Marxist Left Review*, 5 (Summer 2003).

16 Robert Castle and Jim Hagan, 'Settlers and the State: the creation of an Aboriginal workforce in Australia', *Aboriginal History*, 22 (1998), p 26.

17 Cited in Fred Magdoff and John Bellamy Foster, *What Every Environmentalist Needs to Know About Capitalism* (New York: Monthly Review Press, 2011), p 39.

18 Reynolds, p 348.

19 Reynolds, p 341.

20 Reynolds, p 325.

21 Reynolds, p 347.

22 James Boyce, *Van Dieman's Land* (Melbourne: Black Inc, 2018), p 85.

23 Reynolds, p 341.

24 Michael Perlman, *The Invention of Capitalism* (Durham: Duke University Press, 2000), p 63.

25 Martin Empson, 'Kill All the Gentlemen': class struggle and change in the English countryside (London: Bookmarks Publications, 2018), p 177.

26 Thomas More, Utopia (London: Dover, 2012), p 9.

27 JM Neeson, Commoners: common right, enclosure and social change in England, 1700–1820 (Cambridge: Cambridge Uni Press, 1993), p 5.

28 Karl Marx, Capital, Volume One: a critique of political economy (London: Penguin, 1990), Chapter 27.

29 John Walliss, The Bloody Code in England and Wales, 1760–1830 (Liverpool: Palgrave Macmillan, 2018), p 1.

30 Charles Phillips, Vacation Thoughts on Capital Punishments (London: Wentworth Press, 1858), p 3.

31 Hillier and O'Lincoln.

32 Humphrys, p 122.

33 EP Thompson, The Making of the English Working Class (London: Victor Gollancz, 1980), p 445.

34 Andreas Malm, Fossil Capital: the rise of steam-power and the roots of global warming (London: Verso, 2016), p 166.

35 Sidney Pollard, 'Factory Discipline in the Industrial Revolution', The Economic History Review, vol. 16, no. 2, 1963, p 254.

36 Pollard, p 268.

37 Pollard, p 258.

38 Reynolds, p 318.

39 HN Nelson, 'Parker, Edward Stone', Australian Dictionary of Biography (Melbourne: Melbourne University Press, 1974), Volume Five.

40 Reynolds, p 318.

41 Perlman, p 122.

42 Pollard, p 255.

43 Pollard, p 255.

44 John Clare, 'The Mores' in Selected Poetry and Prose (London: Taylor and Francis, 2013), p 92.

45 Mark Maslin and Simon Lewis, 'Why the Anthropocene Began with European Colonisation, Mass Slavery and the "Great Dying" of the 16th Century', Conversation, 25 June 2020.

Chapter Four: The Water Wheel and the Iron Man

1   Mary Shelley, *Frankenstein* (New York: Bantem Dell, 2003), p 38.

2   David McNally, *Monsters of the Market: zombies, vampires, and global capitalism* (Leiden: Brill, 2011), p 99.

3   The argument here draws in part of my article 'Sinister Automatons', *Counterpunch*, 1 November 2012. See also Russell Smith, 'Frankenstein in the Automatic Factory', *Nineteenth-Century Contexts*, 41.3 (2019), pp 303–19.

4   Andrew Ure, 'An Account of some Experiments made on the Body of a Criminal Immediately after Execution, with Physiological and Practical Observations', *Journal of Science and the Arts*, 6 (1819) pp 283–94.

5   McNally, p 25.

6   Charles Z Wallace, 'The Value of the Dead: the commodification of corpses in Western culture', *Spectrum*, 7.1 (2018).

7   Lisa Rosner, *The Anatomy Murders* (Philadelphia: University of Pennsylvania Press, 2011), p 246.

8   McNally, p 53.

9   Peter Berresford-Ellis and Seumas Mac A'Ghobhainn, *The Radical Rising: the Scottish insurrection of 1820* (Edinburgh: Birlinn, 1989).

10 Andrew Ure, 'An Account'.

11 Andrew Ure, *The Philosophy of Manufactures: or, an exposition of the scientific, moral and commercial economy of the factory system of Great Britain* (London: Charles Knight, 1835), p 301.

12 Andreas Malm, *Fossil Capital: the rise of steam-power and the roots of global warming* (London: Verso, 2016), p 245.

13 Ure, *Philosophy*, p 15.

14 Ure, *Philosophy*, p 369.

15 Ure, *Philosophy*, p 368.

16 Ure, *Philosophy*, p 13.

17 Ure, *Philosophy*, p 367.

18 Ure, *Philosophy*, p 370.

19 Malm, p 128.

20 Malm, p 89.

21 Malm, p 264.

22   Malm, p 118.

23   Malm, p 152.

24   Ure, *Philosophy*, p 55.

25   Ure, *Philosophy*, p 18.

26   Malm, p 237.

27   Alexis de Tocqueville, *Journeys to England and Ireland* (New Haven: Yale University Press, 1958), pp 104–7.

28   Dana Thomas, *Fashionopolis: the price of fast fashion and the future of clothes* (New York: Penguin, 2019), p 84.

29   Malm, p 191.

30   Friedrich Engels, *The Condition of the Working Class in England in 1844* (Oxford: Oxford University Press, 2009), p 59.

31   Malm, p 180.

32   See McNally, Chapter One.

33   Shelley, p 158.

34   Malm, p 237.

35   See Stephen Mosley, *The Chimney of the World: a history of smoke pollution in Victorian and Edwardian Manchester* (Abingdon: Routledge, 2008).

Chapter Five: Father Abraham versus Mrs Consumer

1   Julia Brucculieri, '16 Of The Most Outrageous Looks From New York Fashion Week', *Huffington Post*, 17 February 2018.

2   Dana Thomas, *Fashionopolis: the price of fast fashion and the future of clothes* (New York: Penguin, 2019), p 21.

3   Raymond Williams, *Keywords: a vocabulary of culture and society* (New York: Oxford University Press, 1976), p 78.

4   Sophus A Reinert, 'The Way to Wealth around the World: Benjamin Franklin and the globalization of American capitalism', *The American Historical Review*, 120.1 (February 2015), p 66.

5   Reinert, p 75.

6   Benjamin Franklin, *The Way to Wealth* (Bedford: Applewood, 1986), p 19.

7   Reinert, p 79.

8   Stuart Ewen and Elizabeth Ewen, *Channels of desire: mass images and the shaping of American consciousness* (New York: McGraw-Hill, 1982), p 163.

9   Ewen and Ewen, p 166.

10   Frederick W Taylor, *The Principles of Scientific Management* (Fairfield: 1st World Library, 2005), p 42.

11   Taylor, p 43.

12   Taylor, p 63.

13   Taylor, p 36.

14   Taylor, p 5.

15   Harry Braverman, *Labor and Monopoly Capital: the degradation of work in the twentieth century* (New York: Monthly Review Press, *1998)*, Chapter Five.

16   Taylor, p 44.

17   Taylor, p 76.

18   Braverman, p 101.

19   Keith Sward, *The Legend of Henry Ford* (New York: Atheneum, 1975), p 48.

20   Lizabeth Cohen, *A Consumers' Republic: the politics of mass consumption in postwar America* (New York: Vintage, 2004), p 41.

21   Christine Frederick, *Selling Mrs Consumer* (New York: The Business Bourse, 1929), p 102.

22   Franklin, p 25.

23   Frederick, p 106.

Chapter Six: Our Life Will Be Disposable

The argument here draws on ideas expressed in Heather Rogers, *Gone Tomorrow: the hidden life of garbage* (New York: New Press, 2005) and in my *Guardian* column, 'Ending over Mending: Planned Obsolescence Is Killing the Planet', *The Guardian*, 16 March 2021.

1   Aldous Huxley, *Brave New World* (New York: Harper Perennial, 2010), p 54.

2   Vance Packard, *The Waste Makers* (London: Longmans, 1961), p 20.

3   Will Steffen, Wendy Broadgate, Lisa Deutsch, Owen Gaffney, and Cornelia Ludwig, 'The Trajectory of the Anthropocene: the great acceleration', *The Anthropocene Review*, 2.1 (2015), pp 81–98.

4   Ian Angus and Simon Butler, *Too Many People?: population, immigration, and the environmental crisis* (Chicago: Haymarket, 2011), p 53.

5   Franklin D Roosevelt, *The public papers and addresses of Franklin D Roosevelt, 1941* (Ann Arbor: University of Michigan Library, 2005), p 6.

6   Tim Trainor, 'How Ford's Willow Run Assembly Plant Helped Win World War II', *Assembly*, 3 January 2019.

7   Packard, p 27.

8   Packard, p 26.

9   Packard, p 27.

10 Alan Phillips, 'Why The Things You Buy Don't Last', *Maclean's*, 17 December 1960, p 13.

11 Rogers, p 114.

12 Packard, p 77.

13 Packard, p 58.

14 Giles Slade, *Made to Break: technology and obsolescence in America* (Cambridge: Harvard University Press, 2006), p 165.

15 Phillips, p 13.

16 Slade, p 151.

17 Ian Angus, 'Barry Commoner and the Great Acceleration', *Climate and Capitalism*, 29 June 2014.

18 Roland Marchand, *Advertising the American Dream: making way for modernity, 1920–1940* (Berkeley: University of California Press, 1985), p 161.

19 Rogers, p 109.

20 Peter Wiles, 'The Soviet Economy Outpaces the West', *Foreign Affairs*, 11 October 2011.

21 Richard Nixon and Nikita Khrushchev, 'The Kitchen Debate – Transcript' *Central Intelligence Agency*, July 1959, <https://www.cia.gov/library/readingroom/docs/1959-07-24.pdf>.

22 Nixon and Khrushchev.

23 Robert Lekachman, 'The Cult of Novelty', *Challenge*, 8.7 (1960), pp 7–11.

24 Christophe Bonneuil and Jean-Baptiste Fressoz, *The Shock of the Anthropocene: the Earth, history, and us* (London: Verso ebook, 2016), Chapter Seven.

25 Packard, p 42.

26 Packard, p 61.

27 Roland Barthes, *Mythologies* (London: Paladin, 1973), p 98.

28 Rogers, p 121.

29 Susan Freinkel, *Plastic: a toxic love story* (Melbourne: Text, 2011), p 142.

30 Jeffrey L Meikle, 'Material Doubts: the consequences of plastic', *Environmental History* 2.3 (1997), p 283.

31 Meikle, pp 283–4.

32 Freinkel, p 143.

33 Freinkel, p 146.

34 Rogers, p 122.

35 'Fact Sheet: How Much Disposable Plastic We Use', *Earth Day Network* (blog), 18 April 2018.

36 Freinkel, p 144.

Chapter Seven: It Looks Like a Green Winter

1 Steve Craig, '"Torches of Freedom": themes of women's liberation in American cigarette advertising, a paper presented to the Gender Studies Division Southwest/Texas', March 1999.

2 Richard Klein, *Cigarettes Are Sublime* (Durham: Duke University Press, 2005), p 135.

3 RT Ravenholt, 'Tobacco's Global Death March', *Population and Development Review*, 16.2 (1990), p 219.

4 Paula S Fass, *The Damned and the Beautiful: American youth in the 1920s* (Oxford: Oxford University Press, 1979), p 295.

5 Larry Tye, *The Father of Spin: Edward L. Bernays and the birth of public relations* (New York: Holt, 2002), p 24.

6   Fass, p 296.

7   Tye, p 34.

8   Tye, p 38.

9   Tye, p 30.

10 Naomi Oreskes and Erik M Conway, *Merchants of Doubt: how a handful of scientists obscured the truth on issues from tobacco smoke to global warming* (New York: Bloomsbury Press, 2011), p 15.

11 Michael J Goodman, 'Tobacco's PR Campaign: the cigarette papers', *Los Angeles Times*, 18 September 1994.

12 Allan M Brandt, 'Inventing Conflicts of Interest: a history of tobacco industry tactics', *American Journal of Public Health*, 102.1 (2012), p 66.

13 Allan M Brandt, *The Cigarette Century: the rise, fall, and deadly persistence of the product that defined America* (New York: Basic Books, 2009), p 182.

14 Brandt, 'Inventing Conflicts of Interest', p 68.

15 Nathaniel Rich, *Losing Earth: a recent history* (New York: Farrar, Straus and Giroux, 2019), p 48.

16 'The Climate Denial Machine: how the fossil fuel industry blocks climate action', *Climate Reality Project*, 5 September 2019.

17 'The Climate Denial Machine'.

18 Damian Carrington and Jelmer Mommers, 'Shell's 1991 Warning: climate changing "at faster rate than at any time since end of ice age"', *The Guardian*, 28 February 2017.

19 Jelmer Mommers and Damian Carrington, 'If Shell knew climate change was dire 25 years ago, why still business as usual today?', *The Correspondent*, 28 February 2017.

20 Oreskes and Conway, p 5.

21 Sara Jerving, Katie Jennings, Masako Melissa Hirsch, and Susanne Rust, 'What Exxon Knew about the Earth's Melting Arctic', *Los Angeles Times*, 9 October 2015.

22 Amy Lieberman and Susanne Rust, 'Big Oil Braced for Global Warming While It Fought Regulations', *Los Angeles Times*, 31 December 2015.

23 Edward L Bernays, *Propaganda* (Brooklyn: Ig Publishing, 2005), p 10.

24 Bernays, p 11.

25 Tye, pp 53–4.

26 Heather Rogers, 'Garbage Capitalism's Green Commerce', *Socialist Register*, 43 (2007), pp 231–53.

27 Keep America Beautiful, 'Susan Spotless', 1961, television public service announcement.

28 Keep America Beautiful, 'Crying Indian', 1971, television public service announcement.

29 Ian Angus, 'Barry Commoner and the Great Acceleration', *Climate and Capitalism*, 29 June 2014.

30 Rogers, p 123.

31 'Thirty Years Later Keep America Beautiful Is Still Keeping America Blindfolded', *Bottle Bill Resource Guide*, Spring 2000.

32 Sharon Beder, 'Ecological Double Agents', *Australian Science*, 19.1 (February 1998), pp 19–22.

33 Laura Sullivan, 'How Big Oil Misled the Public into Believing Plastic Would Be Recycled', *NPR*, 11 September 2020.

34 Sullivan.

35 Erin McCormick, Bennett Murray, Carmela Fonbuena, Leoni Kijewski, Gökçe Saraçoğlu, Jamie Fullerton, Alastair Gee, and Charlotte Simmonds, 'Where Does Your Plastic Go? Global investigation reveals America's dirty secret', *The Guardian*, 17 June 2019.

36 Julie Doyle, 'Where has all the oil gone? BP branding and the discursive elimination of climate change risk' in Nick Heffernan and David E Wragg, eds., *Culture, Environment and Ecopolitics* (Newcastle upon Tyne: Cambridge Scholars Publishing, 2011), pp 200–225.

37 Mark Kaufman, 'The Devious Fossil Fuel Propaganda We All Use', *Mashable*, 26 April 2021.

38 Timothy Gutowski et al., 'Environmental Lifestyle Analysis (ELSA)', *2008 IEEE International Symposium on Electronics and the Environment*, 2008, pp 1–5.

Chapter Eight: The World's Worst Wound

Some of this argument appeared in a *Guardian* column: 'Climate Change Is a Disaster Foretold, Just like the First World War', *The Guardian*, 12 March 2018.

1   Elizabeth Kolbert, *Field Notes from a Catastrophe: man, nature, and climate change* (New York: Bloomsbury, 2006), p 187.

2   Asher Moses, '"Collapse of Civilisation Is the Most Likely Outcome": top climate scientists', *Voice of Action*, 8 June 2020.

3   John Keegan, *The First World War* (New York: Knopf, 1999), p 17.

4   John Bellamy Foster and Brett Clark, 'The Paradox of Wealth: capitalism and ecological destruction', *Monthly Review*, 1 November 2009.

5   James Maitland, *An Inquiry into the Nature and Origin of Public Wealth, and into the Means and Causes of Its Increase by the Earl of Lauderdale* (Edinburgh: Archibald Constable & Co, 1819).

6   Erin Durkin, 'Shocking Autopsy Photos Show Toll of Plastic Waste on Dead Whale', *The Guardian*, 19 March 2019.

7   'About', *Alliance to End Plastic Waste,* <https://endplasticwaste.org/en/about>

8   Sandra Laville, 'Founders of Plastic Waste Alliance "Investing Billions in New Plants"', *The Guardian*, 21 January 2019.

9   Matthew Taylor, '$180bn Investment in Plastic Factories Feeds Global Packaging Binge', *The Guardian*, 26 December 2017.

10 Richard York and Shannon Bell, 'Energy Transitions or Additions?', *Energy Research & Social Science*, 51 (2019), pp 40–3.

11 REN21, *Renewables 2020 Global Status Report* (Paris: REN21 Secretariat, 2020).

12 William Stanley Jevons, *The Coal Question* (London: Macmillan, 1865), p 103.

13 David Owen, 'The Efficiency Dilemma', *The New Yorker*, 13 December 2010.

14 T Vadén, V Lähde, A Majava, P Järvensivu, T Toivanen, and JT Eronen, 'Raising the Bar: on the type, size and timeline of a "successful" decoupling', *Environmental Politics*, 30.3 (2021), pp 462–76.

15 Damian Carrington, 'World's Consumption of Materials Hits Record 100bn Tonnes a Year', *The Guardian*, 22 January 2020.

16 European Environmental Bureau (EEB), ed., 'Decoupling Debunked. Evidence and arguments against green growth as a sole strategy for sustainability', *EEB*, 8 July 2019.

17 Olivia Carville, '"We Needed to Go": rich Americans activate pandemic escape plans', *Bloomberg*, 19 April 2020.

18 Jason Paul, 'Elon Musk Says Ticket to Mars Will Cost $500,000', *Wired*, 21 March 2012; Kenneth Chang, 'Jeff Bezos Unveils Blue Origin's Vision for Space, and a Moon Lander', *The New York Times*, 9 May 2019.

19 Marie Boran, 'Nanobots will live in our brains in the 2030s, says Google boss', *The Irish Times*, 19 May 2017.

Chapter Nine: The Great Race

1 J Drew Lanham, 'Nine New Revelations for the Black American Bird-Watcher', *Vanity Fair*, 27 May 2020.

2 Candice Pires, '"Bad Things Happen in the Woods": the anxiety of hiking while Black', *The Guardian*, 13 July 2018.

3 Alexis de Tocqueville, *Democracy in America* (Chicago: University of Chicago Press, 2000), Chapter 17.

4 Paul Outka, *Race and Nature from Transcendentalism to the Harlem Renaissance* (New York: Palgrave Macmillan, 2008), p 29.

5 Emma Marris, *Rambunctious Garden: saving nature in a post-wild world* (New York: Bloomsbury, 2013), p 22.

6 Jonathan Spiro, *Defending the Master Race: conservation, eugenics, and the legacy of Madison Grant* (Burlington: University of Vermont Press, 2009), p 4.

7 Spiro, p 29.

8 Paul Krausman and Shane P Mahoney, 'How the Boone and Crockett Club (B&C) Shaped North American Conservation', *International Journal of Environmental Studies* 72.5 (September 2015), p 748.

9 Spiro, p 55.

10 John Hutgren, *Border Walls Gone Green* (Minneapolis: University of Minnesota Press, 2015), p 37.

11 Hutgren, p 37.

12 Gray Brechin, 'Conserving the Race: natural aristocracies, eugenics, and the U.S. conservation movement', *Antipode* 28.3 (1996), p 236.

13 Madison Grant, *The Passing of the Great Race* (New York: Scribner, 1936), p 127.

14 Spiro, p xii.

15 Spiro, p 385.

16 Laura Dassow Walls, *Henry David Thoreau: A Life* (Chicago: University of Chicago Press, 2017), p 444.

17 Karl Jacoby, *Crimes Against Nature: squatters, poachers, thieves, and the hidden history of American conservation* (Berkeley: University of California Press, 2001), p 86.

18 Jacoby, p 87.

19 See Jacoby, p 151.

20 Spiro, p 3.

21 Adam Rome, 'Nature Wars, Culture Wars: immigration and environmental reform in the progressive era', *Environmental History* 13.3 (2008), p 434.

22 Rome, p 437.

23 Joseph E Taylor III and Matthew Klingle, 'Environmentalism's Elitist Tinge Has Roots in the Movement's History', *Grist*, 9 March 2006.

24 Rome, p 445.

25 Peter Staudenmaier, 'Fascist Ecology: the "Green Wing" of the Nazi Party and its historical antecedents', in Janet Biehl and Peter Staudenmaier, eds., *Ecofascism Revisited: lessons from the German experience* (Porsgrunn: New Compass Press, 2011), pp 9–34.

26 Spiro, p 97.

27 Garland E Allen, '"Culling the Herd": eugenics and the conservation movement in the United States, 1900–1940', *Journal of the History of Biology*, 46.1 (2013), pp 31–72.

Chapter Ten: People, People, People

1   Thomas Malthus, *An Essay on the Principle of Population: the 1803 edition* (New Haven: Yale University Press, 2018), Chapter VI.

2   Marcus, *The Book of Murder!* (London: John Hill, 1839).

3   John Bellamy Foster, 'Malthus Essay on Population at Age 200', *Monthly Review*, 1 Dec 1998.

4   Adam Rome, 'The Genius of Earth Day', *Environmental History*, 15.2 (April 2010), pp 194–205.

5   Adam Rome, '"Give Earth a Chance": the environmental movement and the Sixties', *The Journal of American History*, 90.2 (September 2003), pp 525–54.

6   Thomas Robertson, *The Malthusian Moment: global population growth and the birth of American environmentalism* (New Brunswick: Rutgers University Press, 2012), p 169.

7   Sebastian Normandin and Sean A Valles, "How a Network of Conservationists and Population Control Activists Created the Contemporary US Anti-Immigration Movement," *Endeavour*, 39.2 (June 2015), p 97.

8   Robertson, p 170.

9   Matthew Connelly, *Fatal Misconception: the struggle to control world population* (Cambridge: Harvard University Press, 2010), p 187.

10 William Vogt, *Road to Survival* (New York: W Sloane Associates, 1948), p 214.

11 Robertson, p 7.

12 Paul R Ehrlich, *The Population Bomb* (New York: Ballantine Books, 1968), p 69.

13 Normandin and Valles, p 97.

14 Robertson, p 117.

15 Robertson, p 4.

16 Vogt, p 34.

17 Robertson, p 2.

18 Ehrlich, p 168.

19 Robertson, p 149.

20 Charles C Mann, 'The Book That Incited a Worldwide Fear of

Overpopulation', *Smithsonian Magazine*, February 2018.

21 Ian Angus and Simon Butler, *Too Many People?: population, immigration, and the environmental crisis* (Chicago: Haymarket Books, 2011), p 12.

22 Ehrlich, p 66.

23 Mann.

24 Angus and Butler, p 111.

25 Paul R Ehrlich, Loy Bilderback, and Anne H Ehrlich, *The Golden Door: international migration, Mexico, and the United States* (New York: Wideview Books, 1981), p xiii.

26 Hutgren, p 69.

27 Normandin and Valles, p 104.

28 'Plastics in the Ocean', *Ocean Conservancy*, 7 March 2017.

29 Susan A Berger, '"Oh, What a Tangled Web We Weave"': the triangulation of environmentalism, population growth, and immigration in the U.S.', *Review of History and Political Science*, 4.2 (2016), p 14.

30 See, for instance, Mahmood Mamdani, *The Myth of Population Control: family, caste, and class in an Indian village* (New York: Monthly Review Press, 1972).

31 Federica Cocco, 'Highest Fertility Rates in Europe Still below "Replenishment Level"', *Financial Times*, 28 March 2018.

32 'World Population Growth Is Expected to Nearly Stop by 2100', *Pew Research Center*, 17 June 2019.

33 An argument explained well in Ian Angus and Simon Butler, *Too Many People?: population, immigration, and the environmental crisis*, on which I have drawn heavily.

34 Vogt, p 34.

35 Robertson, p 174.

36 Connelly, p 259.

Chapter Eleven: War on Nature

1 Amanda Lohrey, *Quarterly Essay 8, Groundswell: the rise of the Greens* (Melbourne: Black Inc, 2002), p 10.

2   Oliver Goldsmith, *The Deserted Village and Other Poems* (London: Phoenix, 1996).

3   'Ernest Jones, Chartist: Poems (2)' <https://minorvictorianwriters.org.uk/jones/c_poems_2.htm#1847_vol1a>.

4   Andreas Malm, *Fossil Capital: the rise of steam -ower and the roots of global warming* (London: Verso, 2016), p 239.

5   The best account of this is Douglas R Weiner, *Models of Nature: ecology, conservation, and cultural revolution in Soviet Russia* (Pittsburgh: University of Pittsburgh Press, 2000).

6   Douglas R Weiner, *A Little Corner of Freedom: Russian nature protection from Stalin to Gorbachev* (Berkeley: University of California Press, 1999), p 45.

7   Arran Gare, 'Soviet Environmentalism', *Historical Materialism*, 5 February 2018.

8   Weiner, *Models of Nature*, p 168.

9   Joshua R Keefe, 'Stalin and the Drive to Industrialize the Soviet Union', *Inquiries Journal*, 1 October 2009.

10 SG Wheatcroft and RW Davies, 'Soviet Industrialization Reconsidered: some preliminary conclusions about economic development between 1926 and 1941', *Economic History Review*, 39.2 (1986), pp 269–94.

11 Arran Gare, 'The Environmental Record of the Soviet Union', *Capitalism Nature Socialism*, 13.3 (2002), p 68.

12 Zhores A Medvedev, 'The Environmental Destruction of the Soviet Union', *Ecologist*, 20.1 (1990), p 24.

13 DJ Peterson, *Troubled Lands: the legacy of Soviet environmental destruction* (Boulder: Westview Press, 1993), p 2.

14 Leopol'd Averbakh, Maxim Gorky, and Semen Georgievich Firin, eds., *Belomor: an account of the construction of the new canal between the White Sea and the Baltic Sea* (Westport: Hyperion Press, 1977), p 306.

15 Anne Applebaum, *Gulag: a history* (New York: Knopf Doubleday Publishing Group, 2007), p 64.

16 Cynthia Ann Ruder, *Making History for Stalin: the story of the Belomor Canal* (Gainesville: University Press of Florida, 1998), p 15.

17   Averbakh, Gorky, and Firin, p 333.

18   Elizabeth Astrid Papazian, *Manufacturing Truth* (DeKalb: Northern Illinois University Press, 2009), p 3.

19   See Katerina Clark, *The Soviet Novel: history as ritual* (Bloomington: Indiana University Press, 2000), p 103.

20   Weiner, p 170.

21   See Judith Shapiro, *Mao's War Against Nature: politics and the environment in revolutionary China* (Cambridge: Cambridge University Press, 2001).

22   Anton Cheremukhin, Mikhail Golosov, Sergei Guriev, and Aleh Tsyvinski, 'Was Stalin Necessary for Russia's Economic Development?', *VoxEU*, 10 October 2013.

23   Rick De Vos, 'Inundation, Extinction and Lacustrine Lives', *Cultural Studies Review*, 25.1 (2019), pp 102–18.

Chapter Twelve: Social Murder

1   Josh Taylor, 'Choking Point: how Australia's bushfires have left its citizens struggling for air', *The Guardian*, 17 January 2020.

2   Nerilie J Abram et al., 'Connections of Climate Change and Variability to Large and Extreme Forest Fires in Southeast Australia', *Communications Earth & Environment*, 2.1 (2021), p 8.

3   B Esplin, A Gill, and N Enright, 'Report of the Inquiry into the 2002–2003 Victorian Bushfires' (Melbourne: State Government of Victoria, 2003), p 19.

4   Lily Van Eeden et al., 'Australia's 2019–2020 Bushfires: the wildlife toll', interim report, 2020.

5   'After the Bushfires: addressing the health impacts', bushfire expert brief, Australian Academy of Health and Medical Sciences and Australian Academy of Science, September 2020.

6   Calla Wahquist, 'Australia's Summer Bushfire Smoke Killed 445 and Put Thousands in Hospital, Inquiry Hears', *The Guardian*, 26 May 2020.

7   Friedrich Engels, *The Condition of the Working Class in England in*

1844 (Oxford: Oxford University Press, 1993), p 107.

8   Pablo Gutiérrez, Ashley Kirk, Jonathan Watts, and Frank Hulley-Jones, 'How Fires Have Spread to Previously Untouched Parts of the World', *The Guardian*, 19 February 2021.

9   James Purtill, 'Heatwaves May Render Parts of Sydney Unliveable in Decades', *ABC*, 23 January 2021.

10 Terri McCormack, 'Kelly's Bush', in *Dictionary of Sydney*, 2008 <http://dictionaryofsydney.org/entry/kellys_bush>.

11 Kim Hunter, 'When Workers Fight For Our Environment', *International Socialism Journal*, 168 (October 2020), <https://isj.org.uk/workers-fight-for-environment/>.

12 See Meredith Burgmann and Verity Burgmann, *Green Bans, Red Union: environmental activism and the New South Wales Builders Labourers' Federation* (Sydney: University of New South Wales Press, 1998), pp 167–247.

13 Burgmann and Burgmann, p 54.

14 Burgmann and Burgmann, p 178.

15 AAP, 'Scott Morrison tells students striking over climate change to be "less activist"', *The Guardian*, 26 November 2018.

16 'Records of the Strike in Egypt under Ramses III, C1157BCE', *Libcom.Org*, <http://libcom.org/history/records-of-the-strike-in-egypt-under-ramses-iii>.

17 Marshall Berman, 'What Does "The Communist Manifesto" Have to Offer 150 Years after Its Publication?', *Nation*, 23 March 2015.

18 Caleb Crain, 'State of the Unions', *The New Yorker*, 19 August 2019.

19 Naomi Klein, 'Climate Time vs The Constant Now' in *On Fire: the burning case for a Green New Deal* (New York: Simon & Schuster, 2019).

20 Louise Raw, *Striking a Light: the Bryant and May matchwomen and their place in labour history* (London: Continuum, 2009), p 9.

21 Raw, p 141.

22 Raw, p 163.

23 Raw, p 155.

24 Jake Alimahomed-Wilson and Ellen Reese, *The Cost of Free Shipping:*

Amazon in the global economy (London: Pluto Press, 2020), p xi.

25   Michael Sainato, '"I'm not a robot": Amazon workers condemn unsafe, grueling conditions at warehouse', *The Guardian*, 5 February 2020.

26   Emily Guendelsberger, 'Part One, Amazon: three weeks to Christmas' in *On the Clock: what low-wage work did to me and how it drives America insane* (New York: Little, Brown and Company ebook, 2019),

27   Guendelsberger, 'Part One, Amazon: one month to Christmas'.

28   Will Evans et al., 'How Amazon Hid its Safety Crisis in Colorado — and Nationwide', *Colorado Sun*, 29 September 2020.

29   Ken Klippenstein, 'Documents Show Amazon Is Aware Drivers Pee in Bottles and Even Defecate En Route, Despite Company Denial', *Intercept*, 26 March 2021.

30   Guendelsberger, 'Part One, Amazon: one month to Christmas'.

31   Alimahomed-Wilson and Reese, p 3.

32   Alimahomed-Wilson and Reese, p 5.

33   Freya Newman and Elizabeth Humphrys, 'Construction Workers in a Climate Precarious World', *Critical Sociology*, 46.4–5 (2020), pp 557–72.

34   Kate Davidson, 'Amazon Workers Describe Heat And Noise At Portland Warehouse', *OPB*, 13 July 2019.

35   Christopher Ingram, 'Jeff Bezos' and Elon Musk's Wealth Skyrocketed during the Pandemic', *The Washington Post*, 19 February 2021.

36   Annie Palmer, 'Amazon Says More than 19,000 Workers Got Covid-19', *CNBC*, 1 October 2020.

37   'Climate and COVID-19: converging crises', *The Lancet*, 397.10269 (2021), p 71.

38   Neela Banerjee, 'Q&A: A Harvard Expert on Environment and Health Discusses Possible Ties Between COVID and Climate', *Inside Climate News*, 12 March 2020.

39   'Impacts of COVID-19 Disproportionately Affect Poor and Vulnerable: UN Chief', *UN*, 30 June 2020.

40   Newman and Humphrys, p 560.

41   Larry Buchanan, Quoctrung Bui, and Jugal K Patel, 'Black Lives

Matter May Be the Largest Movement in U.S. History', *The New York Times*, 3 July 2020.

42 'George Floyd: what happened in the final moments of his life', *BBC News*, 16 July 2020.

43 Michelle Alexander, *The New Jim Crow: mass incarceration in the age of colorblindness* (New York: New Press, 2012), p 3.

44 Nathan Robinson, 'The Shocking Finding From the DOJ's Ferguson Report That Nobody Has Noticed', *Huffpost*, 13 May 2015.

45 Mary Ward, 'Jack Mundey Dies Aged 90', *The Sydney Morning Herald*, 11 May 2020.

46 Burgmann and Burgmann, p 250.

47 Hunter.

48 Verity Burgmann, *Power, Profit and Protest: Australian social movements and globalisation* (Sydney: Allen and Unwin, 2003), p 170.

49 Elizabeth Anderson and Stephen Macedo, *Private Government: how employers rule our lives (and why we don't talk about it)* (Oxford: Princeton University Press, 2017), p 37.

50 Guendelsberger, 'Conclusion: out of the weeds'.

51 Sarah Jaffe, *Work Won't Love You Back: how devotion to our jobs keeps us exploited, exhausted, and alone* (New York: Bold Type Books ebook, 2021), Introduction.

Chapter Thirteen: News from Somewhere

1 A point made very strongly in John Bellamy Foster, *The Return of Nature: socialism and ecology* (New York: Monthly Review Press, 2020).

2 José A Tapia Granados, 'Commentary: William Ogburn, Dorothy Thomas and the influence of recessions and expansions on mortality', *International Journal of Epidemiology*, 44.5 (2015), pp 1484–90.

3 Joseph Eyer, 'Prosperity as a Cause of Death', *International Journal of Health Services: Planning, Administration, Evaluation*, 7.1 (1977), pp 125–50.

4 *Paul Mattick*, 'Health and Economic Crises in Conversation with

José Tapia, *Brooklyn Rail*, October 2014.

5   Mark Fisher, *Capitalist Realism: is there no alternative?* (Winchester: Zero Books, 2009), p 17.

6   Ralph Chami, Thomas Cosimano, Connel Fullenkamp, and Sena Oztosun, 'Nature's Solution to Climate Change', *Finance and Development*, 56.4 (December 2019), pp 34–8.

7   Chami et al, p 37.

8   Alex Callinicos, *An Anti-Capitalist Manifesto* (Malden: Blackwell Publishers, 2003), p 116.

9   William Morris, 'Architecture and History', speech delivered *1 July 1884* at the annual meeting held at the Society of Arts, Adelphi Street, Adelphi, London, <https://www.marxists.org/archive/morris/works/1884/spab10.htm>.

10   Foster, p 93.

11   Edward Bellamy, *Looking Backward* (New York: Dover Publications, 1996).

12   Bellamy, p 115.

13   EP Thompson, *William Morris: romantic to revolutionary* (Oakland: PM Press, 2011), p 688.

14   Foster, p 104.

15   'Global Military Expenditure Sees Largest Annual Increase in a Decade — Says SIPRI — Reaching \$1917 Billion in 2019, *SIPRI*, 27 April 2020.

16   A Guttman, 'Advertising Market Worldwide — Statistics & Facts', *Statista*, 15 January 2021.

17   See Chris Williams, *Ecology and Socialism: solutions to capitalist ecological crisis* (Chicago: Haymarket Books, 2010), p 215.

18   Naomi Klein, 'Capitalism vs the Climate' in *On Fire: the burning case for a Green New Deal* (New York: Simon & Schuster, 2019).

19   'Worldwide Food Waste | ThinkEatSave', *UN Environment* <https://www.unenvironment.org/thinkeatsave/get-informed/worldwide-food-waste>; 'World Hunger: key facts and statistics 2021', *Action Against Hunger* <https://www.actionagainsthunger.org/world-hunger-facts-statistics>.

20 For more on this, see Callinicos, p 122, and PJ Devine, *Democracy and Economic Planning: the political economy of a self-governing society* (Cambridge: Polity Press, 1988).

21 Devine, p 33.

22 Stephen Broadberry and Peter Howlett, 'Lessons Learned? British Mobilization for the Two World Wars', in Jari Eloranta et al, eds., *Economic History of Warfare and State Formation* (Singapore: Springer Singapore, 2016).

23 Devine, p 30.

24 JE Lovelock, *The Vanishing Face of Gaia: a final warning* (Camberwell: Penguin Books, 2009), p 94.

25 Devine, p 34.

26 Thompson, p 101.

27 'The Worker's Share of Art', *Commonweal*, I.3 (April 1885), <https://www.marxists.org/archive/morris/works/1885/commonweal/04-workers-art.htm.>

28 William Morris, *News from Nowhere* (London: Routledge, 2017), p 78.

29 Daniel H Pink, *Drive: the surprising truth about what motivates us* (New York: Riverhead Books, 2011).

30 George Orwell, *Why I Write* (New York: Penguin Books, 2005).

31 Morris, p 154.

32 David Laibman, 'The Future within the Present: seven theses for a robust twenty-first-century socialism', *Review of Radical Political Economics*, 38.3 (2006), pp 305–18.

33 Michael A Lebowitz, *The Socialist Alternative: real human development* (New York: Monthly Review Press, 2010), p 43.

34 Foster, p 147.

35 Morris, p 182.

Conclusion: Make Hope Great Again

1 A point made in Emma Marris, *Rambunctious Garden: saving nature in a post-wild world* (New York: Bloomsbury, 2013).

2   Matthew Taylor and Jonathan Watts, 'Revealed: the 20 firms behind a third of all carbon emissions', *The Guardian*, 9 October 2019.

3   Percy Shelley, 'The Mask of Anarchy' in *The Selected Poetry & Prose of Shelley* (Ware: Wordsworth Editions, 1994), p 387.